Sookie

Debbie imagines CK is today, waiting for her to catch some yellow 'hoppers so they can fish together again.

"Sookie," by Deborah Burns Eng and Charles Kellar Burns, Jr. ISBN 978-1-63868-004-8 (hardcover).

Published 2021 by Virtualbookworm.com Publishing, P.O. Box 9949, College Station, TX 77842, US. © 2021, Deborah Burns Eng and Charles Kellar Burns, Jr. All rights reserved. No part of this publication may be reproduced, stored in a retrieval system, or transmitted in any form or by any means, electronic, mechanical, recording or otherwise, without the prior written permission of Deborah Burns Eng and Charles Kellar Burns, Jr.

Table of Contents

Preface

This is the story of CK Burns, the first of several CK's, written by his children, Deborah Burns Eng and CK Burns Jr. We took on this work for two primary reasons: firstly, because we believe that CK was an exemplary human being whose life can serve as a lesson for all of us in how best to live, and secondly, because we hope this narrative will breathe a bit of life into his story for his grandchildren and great grandchildren, none of whom had the honor of knowing him.

We believe that there are people in the world who are extraordinary, ordinary human beings. These are not people whose accomplishments are remembered through centuries; rather, they are people who work to improve the world in small increments, one action or one person at a time. In CK's case, he worked one student, one child, at a time, fostering for them an education, a sense of worth and self-respect, and offering them a path forward in the world. It was the very great good fortune of CK's children to experience him in action and to witness his goodness. We hope that his descendants can catch a glimpse of his sterling example about how to live a life.

Childhood

The manner in which Celia Ann Kelly and Charles Napoleon Burns met is now unknown. Her family spent time in the towns of Valley Mills and Goldthwaite, Texas while his had ties to the Dahlonega and Lumpkin County, Georgia region. Inferentially, it appears that Charlie's family moved to Texas sometime between his birth in Porter Springs, Georgia in 1883 and 1888 when his sister Jenny was born in Texas.

We do know that Celia Ann's father, Daniel Stewart "Doc" Kelly, migrated to Texas after the Civil War and clerked in a drug store in Valley Mills. According to his granddaughter, later he opened his own drug store there and then, moved to Goldthwaite to raise cattle. While he resided in Valley Mills, he married fifteen-year-old Amanda Tennessee McKenzie whose parents operated a wagon yard and travelers' stop for meals and mail handling. Family legend has it that Celia met Charlie in the wagon yard while on a visit from Goldthwaite to see her McKenzie grandparents, an explanation that seems entirely plausible.

While the details of their introduction and courtship shall remain a mystery, we do know that in December, 1908, they married in Bosque County,

Texas, presumably residing in Valley Mills, Texas. Celia Ann would have been almost eighteen years old when she married, and Charlie would have been twenty-five years old.

Wedding Photo of Charlie & Celia

The Burns family soon began to grow. The eldest child, Wallace Morris, was born in 1910, followed by Charles Kellar in 1912, and Daniel Boyd in 1915. It is likely that CK was named for either his father or for a paternal great grandfather, Charles and Napoleon Bonaparte Tankersley, and for an uncle by marriage, Kellar Bonds, the husband of Charlie's sister, Jenny.

Burns Brothers

The family was also increased by the addition of CK's cousin, Evesta "Skeet" Kelly. Skeet and her sister June were the children of Harvey, one of Celia's brothers. Their mother died at an early age while the girls were children. Harvey either would not or could not care for them so their aunts provided a home for them. Skeet lived with Aunt Celia and June lived with Aunt Pearl.

It is difficult to imagine that the family had an easy time making ends meet. Charlie had had to leave school after the second grade in order to help his family, and although he

CK and Celia

later returned as an adult and completed the seventh grade, clearly he had little formal education. A father with little education and no prestigious profession coupled with the effects of the Great Depression beginning in 1929, would surely have made things difficult for the Burns family. Written records and family history indicate that Charlie worked steadily although not at lucrative endeavors. One researcher into family history noted that he would work at any kind of job including janitorial and yard work. There is evidence that Charlie worked for the Depression-era Works Progress Administration in the construction of public works.

Charlie worked as an employee of the Gatesville state school which was a reformatory for boys from 1936 until his death in 1941. There is at least one family story that suggests Charlie worked there as a guard. It was said that on occasion Charlie would place a piece of chalk on an inmate's head and then use a whip to knock it off. Notwithstanding this story, Charlie's death certificate lists him as working for the Gatesville state school as a carpenter, something that seems much more suited to his experience and skills.

Prior to his work at the reformatory, CK's dad, Pap, worked as the custodian of the Valley Mills cemetery from 1907 until 1936, taking the job shortly before his marriage to Celia. He also worked as a grave digger there, and CK mentioned that

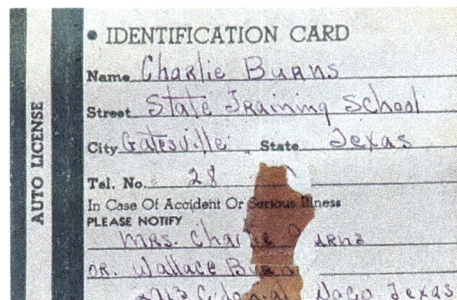

Gatesville ID Card

on occasion the boys had to help with the grave digging, no doubt a burdensome task on a cold day with hard ground. As long as about twenty years after Charlie's death in 1941, a message he painted on a tin shed in the cemetery was still visible. I always marveled at that message as some sort of tangible connection to the grandfather I never knew.

Charlie also worked as a construction foreman and carpenter. As attested to by a plaque recognizing his work on the project, he served as the foreman in the construction of the public school in Valley Mills which is now used as an elementary school campus. According to CK, despite his lack of formal education, Charlie was a very intelligent man. CK noted that Pap

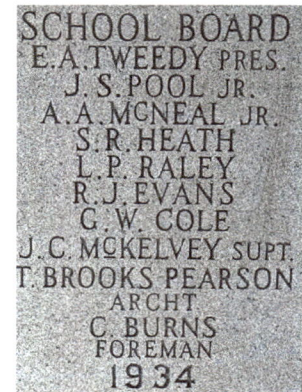

SCHOOL BOARD
E.A. TWEEDY PRES.
J. S. POOL JR.
A. A. MCNEAL JR.
S. R. HEATH
L. P. RALEY
R. J. EVANS
G. W. COLE
J. C. MCKELVEY SUPT.
T. BROOKS PEARSON
ARCHT
C. BURNS
FOREMAN
1934

VM School Plaque

could accurately estimate the construction materials required for any kind of job.

Pap Burns

Family lore has it that Charlie was physically imposing, perhaps standing as tall as six feet six inches which would have made him a giant for that time. He was said on occasion to walk around Valley Mills carrying a much smaller man on his shoulders.

In Valley Mills, the family resided in a modest house on the west side of Highway 317 just before one crossed over the railroad tracks to enter the town. When CK's family lived there, there was a cut in the limestone formation so that traffic dipped down to cross over the tracks which meant that the Burns

8

house was elevated above the level of the highway and the railroad tracks. In later years when CK lived in Crawford and would drive to Valley Mills to visit his mother or his brother Wallace, we children would often sing out "there's where daddy used to live" when we passed by the house.

CK and Pap at boyhood home

It seems likely that the railroad cut may have afforded the three brothers a place to explore and play as well. It may be that CK was first exposed to buckeyes while wandering along the railroad track. He considered buckeyes to be good luck charms and carried some with him even in adult life, particularly during basketball season.

CK related the story that when the family resided there, they had a woman who came each week to wash the family's clothes. Given the time, the washing would no doubt have taken place outdoors using large wash pots. The brothers sometimes climbed on top of an adjacent shed and tossed small rocks into the wash water to annoy the washer woman.

CK attended school in Valley Mills, graduating in May of 1930. His report cards indicate that his attendance was excellent and that he was an above average student. His third-grade teacher did admonish him in one monthly report on his report card to "work harder."

CK's Report Card

Presumably, the Burns family attended the Methodist Church in Valley Mills when CK was growing up. We do know that Celia attended there in later years as she was able. Likewise, we know that CK and his older brother Wallace were in good enough standing as Sunday School attendees to garner spots on a church-sponsored trip to the Ft. Worth Fat Stock Show in March of 1925.

Athletics

CK was always a good athlete and apparently that was the case during his school days in Valley Mills. There is tangible proof of his prowess in the form of a UIL tennis medal, his subsequent collegiate football career, and the testimony of his wife, Marj. According to her, while in high school, in either 1928 or 1929, CK and his doubles partner, Lane Barnett, qualified for the state tennis tournament in Austin. Unfortunately, the right to play for a state championship did not carry with it transportation to the tournament. CK, and presumably Lane, hitchhiked to the tournament from Valley Mills. Despite the fact that they were beaten and eliminated prior to the championship match, it is still a remarkable story. For example, if they had no money for transportation, did they have funds for food and lodging? And, if they had to hitchhike, it would have been prudent to have allowed extra time in order to be sure they arrived in time for their match. That might have meant sleeping rough in Austin to be certain of being on time or arriving just prior to the match but tired from thumbing rides to the tournament. Just to get to Austin was a remarkable accomplishment--and not only did they manage to get to the tournament, but photos show them looking quite dapper in their tennis whites. CK continued to play tennis subsequent to high school and, among other honors, won the tennis championship at the Mare Island Naval Base when he was stationed there at the end of World War II.

State Tournament

Tennis was hardly CK's only sport. He was a proficient enough golfer to own a set of left-handed clubs, and for some years, both before and after World War II, he played semi-professional baseball in central Texas. I never saw him play tennis or golf; I have always assumed that was because the necessary facilities for those two sports were not readily available in the Crawford area where CK's family lived. It is difficult to imagine where a young man of modest means living in Valley Mills may have developed an interest in golf, but his interest in tennis could have been fostered by the two tennis courts adjacent to the Valley Mills school when CK lived there.

I do vaguely remember watching him play baseball. The games that I recall were played on what is now the Crawford High School football field in Tonkawa Park. At that time, the current football field was in the process of conversion from a riding arena to a football field and left much to be desired as a baseball field. I recall that CK played first base. He threw right-handed and batted left-handed. I remember a game in which he had to slide into second base. His slide may have been successful, but in the process he acquired a huge strawberry friction burn on his hip. That injury may have sent him a

12

message that his playing days were waning--he would have been about forty years old at that time.

Apparently CK had a history of sorts about sliding into second base while playing baseball. In one of his wartime letters to his wife, he mentioned that he had injured himself sliding into second base on a coral baseball field. Even assuming the coral was crushed, that had to have been painful.

Despite an absence of information about CK's high school football career we can surmise that he was an excellent player since he played four years while in college. His first stop was at Weatherford Junior College in Weatherford, Texas for the 1930 football season. Subsequent to that he played the 1936 through 1938 seasons at the University of North Texas and served as a co-captain his senior year. The college yearbook for 1939 mentions him repeatedly in its narratives of the season's games and also states that he received all-conference recognition at the end of the year. He had also received all-conference recognition for the 1937 season.

In accordance with the practice of the time, CK played the end position on both offense and defense. He was sometimes referred to as the "elongated end" because of his height, and I had always assumed he was renowned for his offensive abilities. However, the school newspaper for UNT, *The Campus Chat,* in its December 8, 1938, edition which named him to the all-conference team, touted his defensive abilities. Regardless of whether he was a better offensive or defensive player, CK must have made a very favorable impression on his teammates to have been elected co-captain.

Weatherford JC Coyotes #30

UNT Eagles - 3rd from right row 3

Coach with CK #68

OFFICIAL PROGRAM

STEPHEN F. AUSTIN STATE TEACHERS COLLEGE
vs NORTH TEXAS STATE TEACHERS COLLEGE

Football Program North Texas State

CK makes the catch

Co Captain North Texas State

14

Apparently CK participated fully in campus life at UNT. In addition to being an important member of the football team, he was the secretary-treasurer of the T-Club letterman's association, a member of the Physical Education Professional Club, and the Geezles social club which he pledged in the spring of 1937. Indeed, CK appears to have been a loyal enough Geezle that after his graduation he returned to Denton for a club banquet escorting the lady of his dreams to show her off.

He also participated in intramural sports in softball, tennis, and basketball. It appears that the intramural teams on which he played were composed of fellow football players. Those teams generally did quite well, and CK was a standout performer. He was also a semi-finalist for the university championship in tennis.

As a PE major, CK was probably expected to assist with various departmental activities, and apparently he fulfilled that obligation. For example, in May, 1937, the Texas Class B state track and field tournament was held at UNT and was officiated by various members and students of the PE Department. CK assisted with the discus and shot put events.

CK's name was mentioned regularly in the University of North Texas student newspaper, *The Campus Chat*. Most of these references were to his athletic endeavors; however, the *Chat* mentioned in August, 1940, that a student named Dorothy Dillon had finally decided between CK and a rival for her favor and was going to marry the other fellow. However, according to CK,

Miss Dillon had previously proposed to him, and he had declined, no doubt because by that time CK was on the verge of serious romantic interest in Marjorie Jones. Presumably, he was not shaken by Miss Dillon's decision, but it is noteworthy that CK was well-known enough to have merited mention after he had graduated and left UNT and that the author of the writing knew enough about him to think that he would not be offended by reference to such a personal matter as his love life.

UNT Activity Card

Education

CK's higher education included course work done at Clifton Junior College, Weatherford Junior College, the University of North Texas, and Baylor University. Consistent with his experiences in Valley Mills, he remained a better than average student. He received a BS degree from UNT with a major in physical education and minors in English and mathematics and 151 semester hours to his credit. Beginning in 1950, he attended Baylor University on a part-time basis and obtained a Master of Education degree in 1952.

After completion of his BS degree in the spring of 1939, CK returned to Valley Mills and accepted a teaching position there. It appears that he had previously taught there during the 1932 through 1936 school years, so a return to the Valley was probably an easy transition for him to make.

CK and VM Class

The Courtship

Upon his return, he quickly encountered Marjorie Jones who would eventually become his wife. Marjorie was originally from Temple, Texas and had recently completed her BA degree from Texas Christian University. The 1939-1940 school year in Valley Mills was her first teaching experience. Marjorie and another unmarried teacher, Loura Fern Brian, boarded with Miss Bessie Nowlin. Later Bessie became a nanny for CK Burns Jr.

VM faculty with CK and Marj

Valley Mills High School 1939

CK and Marj met in the bookroom at the Valley Mills school according to family legend. They were both handsome, witty, and intelligent people so it is not difficult to imagine that each was impressed with the other. Marjorie was twenty-three at that time. She was a slender brunette with beguiling eyes and a dazzling smile who had been pursued by a number of ardent admirers prior to her encounter with Mr. Burns. In fact, she had briefly been engaged prior to her arrival in Valley Mills. For his part, CK was about six feet three inches tall with dark wavy hair, a dimpled chin, eyes that were blue with gray (so said Marj), and an equally brilliant smile, especially for Miss Jones.

Not only were they both impressive people, but their courtship became more likely given that opportunities for socializing with other people of the same age were likely rather limited in Valley Mills. One can easily imagine CK pulling up to the front door of Bessie Nowlin's boarding house in his Chevrolet "Little 85" coupe to call upon Miss Jones in Bessie's front parlor for an evening of popcorn and flirtation.

Marjorie Jones

As the romance progressed, it was natural that Marj would want to introduce the handsome and charming CK to her social circle and family. One such opportunity arose when her cousin Mildred Cabiness visited her in Valley Mills. Apparently Marj had set the stage for Mildred by extolling CK's many

C.K. Burns

virtues before Mildred met him. When she laid eyes upon him, she simply shrieked, "Sookie" and greeted him effusively. As it turned out, Mildred had met CK previously during college at North Texas. Mildred graduated as a PE major in June of 1938, and she had been a member of the UNT Green Jackets which was a service and spirit organization for the university. Undoubtedly the paths of Mildred and CK had crossed, and there is little doubt that she knew him well enough to use a nickname that few people knew and that even fewer used. According to Mildred, Marj was a bit miffed that her surprise did not turn out quite as she had planned. Mildred delighted in telling this story her entire life, and Marjorie usually seemed slightly annoyed when that happened.

Marj related a story of her own about how she came to be involved with her handsome fellow teacher. One day there was an assembly program scheduled so everyone gathered in the auditorium. What Miss Jones did not know was that the program was to be a debate on which of three eligible female teachers CK should date. According to Marjorie, in regard to her, the debaters noted, "Now she doesn't wear much makeup, therefore she looks about as good at the end of the day as she did at the beginning," among other observations. At the end of the debate, Miss Jones was selected as the best match for CK. It is not known what he thought about the program, but Marj noted that soon after this incident, they had their first date.

Despite the fact that Marj was disappointed that CK did not kiss her on the first date, apparently he soon made up for that lost opportunity, and the romance progressed relatively smoothly and quickly. During the summer of 1940, the couple corresponded frequently while they both resided with their parents, she in Temple and he in Gatesville. Despite the fact that CK repeatedly wrote to "Jones" that he loved her, and even sent a graph showing the increase in his feelings for her, the couple did not see a great deal of each other that summer. Perhaps that was because Marj spent part of her summer as a camp counselor or because there may have been some informal Jones family expectations that had to be met such that a suitor could not simply drop in without prior arrangements. There is some indication from correspondence that Marj's mother kept a close eye on the relationship by monitoring the frequency with which CK wrote; however, there is no clear sign that she disapproved of it. CK does mention marriage in passing in his letters, but one cannot tell precisely how serious he was. Marj apparently at some point talked about waiting three years, but one cannot tell whether she was floating a trial balloon or simply teasing. From CK's letters it appears that he spent a lot of his summer playing baseball and scheming how he could spend time with his girl. He did manage to meet her older sister Dorothy and noted that he had met the entire family save for Mildred's dad. For her part, Marj paid the Burns family a visit in Gatesville and thoroughly charmed CK's parents, particularly Pap, who always seemed delighted when Marj sent him a note or greeting.

Correspondence from CK to Marj in the summer of 1941 was a repeat of that of the previous year. CK was clearly, seriously, in love with Marjorie Jones. During that summer of 1941, Marj lived with her family in Temple while CK lived and worked in Valley

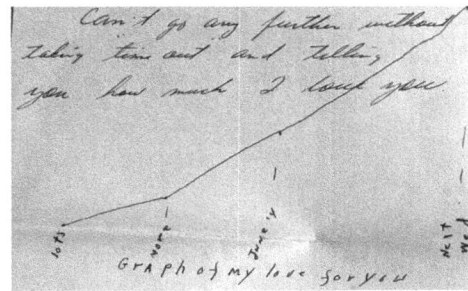

Love Graph

Mills, or as he frequently referred to it, "the Valley." The couple wrote daily with much of their correspondence concerned with their future plans and their financial situation.

As revealed in their letters, the couple had several issues to consider as they carefully moved forward toward marriage. While they abstained from using the "M" word in their writing, it is clear that marriage was their ultimate goal. CK undoubtedly felt pressure to get some money together. He would not have relished the prospect of asking Harry Jones for his daughter's hand in marriage without being fully confident that he could support her--not the least because Harry would likely have inquired about that. CK's effort to acquire a modest nest egg was undercut by the necessity of providing for his recently widowed mother. In essence, CK was attempting to build his mother a house in which to live, to work a second construction job to earn money for marriage, and to court Miss Jones in Temple at every opportunity, all of which made for a daunting summer.

For her part, Marjorie was apparently fending off her mother's suggestion that she seek a teaching job in Temple. Presumably a move to Temple would have afforded more income, greater prestige, and brought her back nearer her parents. Of course, it would also have moved her away from CK, and she had no intention of allowing that to happen.

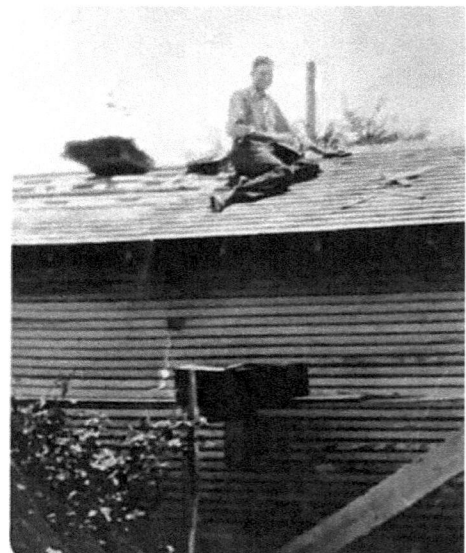

C.K. roofing to raise money for wedding

There are also indications in their correspondence that the couple was cognizant of the likelihood that eventually the U. S. would be drawn into World War II and that such an event would complicate marriage plans enormously.

Eventually CK proposed marriage, and Marjorie accepted with a wedding envisioned for December of 1941. The circumstances of CK's proposal are unknown, but there is some indication that it may have occurred in April, 1941.

The engaged couple's plans were nearly undone by an unfortunate event that occurred in August of 1941. Marj had returned to her home in Temple for the summer, and CK was in the habit of visiting her over as much of a weekend as he could carve out from his construction work. About midnight on Saturday, August 24, as CK was returning to the Valley, he was involved in an accident. He was just south of McGregor on Highway 317 when a car passed him and ran head-on into an approaching vehicle. According to CK, there was plenty of room for the car to have returned to the right-hand lane, but it failed to do so. It rolled over about six times, ejecting the driver, James Feno Jones, who was killed. Mr. Jones' passenger escaped unharmed. The vehicle Jones hit spun into CK's beloved "85" doing serious damage to the little Chevrolet coupe.

Little 85

Fortunately, CK was physically unscathed; however, the accident cost him about $1800 in 2021 dollars to repair his car. He wrote to Marj the day after the wreck and asked her to lend him $100, which of course she did, but undoubtedly the money came from what the couple had saved for wedding and honeymoon expenses.

The Wedding

Marriage would solve one major problem and create an even larger one in its stead. At that time, the Valley Mills school district had a policy that two married people could not both teach in Valley Mills at the same time. Presumably, there was no prohibition against two teachers dating, but as their relationship grew ever more serious, CK and Marj thought it advisable to keep the seriousness of their relationship a secret from most people. Marriage would enable them to be open about their relationship, but they could not both teach in Valley Mills. One can speculate that perhaps a December 21 wedding date was chosen to afford time for a short honeymoon followed by relocation to new teaching jobs at mid-year. Whether planned or not, that is how the situation played out. The couple married in a small ceremony held in the front parlor of Marjorie's childhood home at 718 South 13th Street in Temple on the afternoon of December 21, 1941--just two weeks after Pearl Harbor. Marj noted in a letter to her parents that CK was "so excited" by all the wedding presents the couple received and that he knew exactly who gave what and that he was very diligent in thanking the givers.

As far as can be ascertained, the wedding date was not affected by the outbreak of World War II. If anything affected the timing of the wedding, it was likely the policy of the Valley Mills school district or the death of CK's father, Charlie. Apparently Charlie's death was relatively sudden. CK remarked in some of his wartime correspondence that his father had become ill in March of

1941. CK also wrote how good his father had been to his sons and asked Marj to see to the maintenance of his gravesite. Charlie died on April 1, 1941, and it is plausible that the wedding might have been fixed for a date that allowed his family some time to recover from his death.

Celia

The death of Pap Burns also created a practical problem in that his widow had neither marketable job skills nor a place to live. Charlie and Celia were living in Gatesville while he worked at the reformatory there at the time of his death; without his income Celia had no means to meet living expenses on her own. Into this financial breach stepped the three Burns brothers. Public records indicate that they purchased a lot at 406 Avenue D in Valley Mills, and according to family stories, they also built there the house in which their mother passed the rest of her life. The brothers built a duplex with the idea in mind that Celia could rent one half of the house to bring in some income. Inferentially, however, it seems that the widow Burns was not keen to have boarders encroaching on her space or in her house. At one point during construction in the summer of 1941, she proposed that the rental space be in the form of a garage apartment. CK noted about that proposal that he would probably have to argue with her about it for a few days.

Later, after the completion of the duplex, Celia decided that there needed to be a door between the two kitchens. When her sons moved too slowly to honor her request, she took a pickax and knocked a hole in the wall separating the two kitchens.

As far as can be determined, despite her sons' plans, Celia seldom took in boarders. There were times during World War II that Marjorie lived with her mother-in-law while she taught school in Valley Mills; however, Marjorie and her mother-in-law got along very well, and no doubt her presence was welcome while Celia grieved for Charlie. Marjorie did make a modest monthly payment to Celia.

Reading between the lines, it seems that CK did most of the work in building his mother's house. Dan apparently lived in Vernon, Texas while Wallace, also known as "Son," had two small children and resided in Waco. CK was the son who was both most available and probably the best worker.

It should be noted that her sons took good care of Celia. Apparently, she never warmed to the idea of taking in renters, and so frequently she was left to live on a small amount of Social Security income from her late husband and gifts from her sons. We

Valley Mills house on D street

assume that all three sons contributed; however, his children always thought that CK contributed the most money in the most reliable fashion. From his letters to his wife during World War II, it is clear that he sent home allotments to both his wife and his mother and that he was very diligent in making sure his allotments were handled properly so that his dependents were taken care of whenever he had a change in his duty station or circumstances. On one occasion in order to obtain a larger allotment for her, he informed the navy that he and Marj provided the primary support for Celia and from the context of that narrative, it seems likely that CK and Marj provided Celia's only support. At another time in 1943 when Marj resided with Celia, CK proposed a payment of $15 per month to his mother for his wife's living quarters. He did point out that while living with his mother, Marj had a private bathroom of her own, something that she had not had while boarding with Bessie Nowlin where there were typically several boarders to share one bathroom with Miss Nowlin.

Further, from his letters to Marj from the south Pacific, it is clear that in addition to providing financial assistance to Celia, CK also asked his wife to keep an eye on his grieving mother, which apparently she did very effectively. From CK's correspondence it is clear that Celia held her daughter-in-law in high regard and enjoyed her company when they lived together.

In addition to cash contributions, CK also provided food for his mother and his uncle Robert Burns who also resided in the Valley. CK was conscientious and faithful in visiting his mother as well. Someone in CK's family made a trip to visit Celia at least weekly and a family member was always available to take Celia to various appointments. According to his daughter, on the day that she was born, CK even drove his mother to Houston to visit his brother Dan who was ill.

CK sometimes enlivened trips to visit his mother by trying to coast to her house. At a certain point along the route to her house, CK would take the car out of gear and try to coast as near to her house as he could. We never knew the purpose of the exercise or how it had arisen, but CK enjoyed it.

The In-Laws

CK also made weekly trips to visit his in-laws, Harry and Louise Jones in Temple. This was usually a family trip made on Sunday afternoons after church. Crawford was about thirty-five miles from Temple so that trip was a bit more of an undertaking than a trip to the Valley. While Harry Jones was at home, CK spent a lot of time talking with his father-in-law while sitting on the front porch. Later, after Harry's death, CK enjoyed going to the movies when in Temple. As I recall, Temple had two movie theaters that could be relied upon to show current feature films. CK particularly enjoyed Westerns, especially those starring John Wayne or Randolph Scott, habitually referred to by CK as Randolph Squat. About the only movies CK refused to watch were those that featured Jimmy Cagney.

El Paso

Subsequent to their wedding in December, 1941, CK and Marj moved to El Paso to teach. They resided at 1016 N. Oregon #3. We know of nothing that made El Paso attractive save for the fact that they could both teach there. Nor is it clear how they knew that or how they knew that jobs were available there save for the likelihood that a large school district would inevitably have some mid-year turnover. CK did mention once that he had had an opportunity to join the football coaching staff in El Paso, presumably at El Paso High School where he taught, so he may have been connected there in some manner. On one occasion he wrote Marj from Austin where he was attending a track meet, most likely the state meet, which would suggest a responsible position within the El Paso coaching fraternity. The *El Paso Times* newspaper on March 5, 1942, noted CK's promotion to B team coach at El Paso High School and stated that he "intends to remain in El Paso permanently." Presumably he went into the navy before advancement in El Paso could come to full fruition.

For her part, Marj taught at Beall Elementary School in central El Paso. That may have been a challenging task for her since she was not trained for teaching elementary grades; however, her principal, Myra Clark, bestowed high praise upon her and tried to induce her to return to Beall in the event that CK was assigned sea duty, and she could not accompany him.

Anchors Away

While El Paso may have provided some novel teaching experiences to the newlyweds, presumably they were happy just being together; however, that situation did not last long. On May 4, 1942, CK's local Bosque County draft board classified him as 1-A, and by June of 1942, he was in the navy. He had previously received draft deferments while in Valley Mills, presumably because he was teaching and because the U. S. was not involved in hostilities at that time. We do not know whether he was drafted or acknowledged the inevitable and enlisted, but it seems doubtful that an ardent young husband would leave his new wife voluntarily.

It appears that CK left by train from Dallas for his initial assignment in Norfolk, Virginia. June 29 seems to have been the day of departure since he wrote to Marj on June 30 that he was a few hours out of Norfolk. The couple borrowed Harry Jones' car for the drive to Dallas where Marj watched from the platform until her husband's train pulled out of the station.

The train trip to Norfolk must have been nerve-wracking for CK, marking as it did the beginning of his life as a sailor. Presumably CK had traveled a little within the United States during his football career, but he probably had not made a trip as long as the Dallas to Norfolk journey. More importantly, CK had no certainty about his fate as a sailor. In 1942, the outcome of the war was still in doubt, and there was no way that CK could have foretold how he would be called upon to participate in that war, nor could he have known how long he would be away from his bride of six months. CK did report to Marj a rumor he had heard on the way to Norfolk that "they hardly ever take married men for sea duty," but rumors were rife and carried little value.

Marj returned to the Valley to live with her mother-in-law and teach. Temple might have seemed like a more logical destination, but we do not know what her thinking was or what factors she considered in making her decision to settle in Valley Mills.

From June through September, 1942, CK was a student in a naval physical training instructor's school in Norfolk, Virginia. This appears to have been an instance when the military actually paid attention to a sailor's background and experience and assigned him to duty commensurate with his skills and work history. Conversely, however, CK wrote that his assignment was based on his heighth, and he mentioned that a football player from East Texas State University against whom he had played was also in his unit. Apparently the navy wanted a cadre of big, athletic men to conduct the physical training of its new recruits.

It seems that CK actually entered the navy as a chief petty officer, that is, as a non-commissioned officer, as opposed to entering on duty as an enlisted seaman as would normally have been the case for a draftee. At least there is no mention of a promotion to chief petty officer in CK's correspondence, and he seems to use the CPO rank from the beginning in his letters to Marj. Perhaps the CPO rank was granted in acknowledgement of CK's college degree and his specialized physical education training.

CK's letters to Marj indicate that the physical training instructor's school could be challenging at times. No doubt that was true given that the course of study seems to have been a combination of tedious basic military training and exhausting physical training. It is clear from CK's comments that a number of students washed out of the program due to physical injuries they incurred during training.

CK provided the following schedule of his days at Norfolk:

4:00 – 5:00 dormitory watch wake

5:00 -6:00 morning run

6:00 – 6:45 eat

6:45- 7:45 clean dorm

7:45 – 10:45 drill

10:45 Eat

11:30-12:30 Air Raid Drill by post

1:00 – 3:45 Drill

3:45 Eat

5:00 Athletic detail – referee ball game for recruits

6:00-7:00 Lecture

9:00 Bed

10:00-11:30 Air Raid Drill

11:30 Bed Again

It appears that he was subject to very long days with little down time.

CK quickly felt the intense sting of separation from his newlywed wife and schemed with his prewar friend Truett Day to bring her and Mrs. Day to Norfolk. Apparently the two young women drove from Texas to Virginia. It appears from his letters that they scavenged a spare tire from the "Little 85" and that they may have begun the trip with extra gasoline that they hustled up before they left Texas. Wartime rationing of things such as rubber and gasoline was in effect, so the young women were only being prudent in trying to prepare for emergencies on the journey.

After completion of his training at Norfolk, CK was assigned to Camp Endicott in Davisville, Rhode Island. His introduction to Camp Endicott was unpleasant in that his unit was confined to the post due to an outbreak of meningitis. CK was not pleased to have Marj at hand and to be unable to be with her. For her part, Marj filled her idle hours with a job at a bank.

18 Dedford Street

CK spent the year from September, 1942, to September, 1943, training Sea Bees at Camp Endicott. Sea Bees were navy construction personnel, and CK taught or supervised their physical training. During this period, Marj was able to be with him in Rhode Island where they resided at 18 Dedford Street in East Greenwich.

Chief Petty Officer

Merry Christmas from Rhode Island

In September, 1943, it was time to go to war; however, for CK, except for being away from his wife, it was a relatively good war. He traveled by train from Rhode Island to Treasure Island Naval Base near San Francisco. Along the way he was able to rendezvous with Marj in Chicago. It is not clear how that occurred, but once they managed to obtain a hotel room, they made some wonderful memories that CK drew upon during the long months in the south Pacific. As CK moved on toward Treasure Island, he was able to send Marj a post card from Ogden, Utah to let her know that the island of New Caledonia would be his first duty station in the Pacific theater.

Apparently once CK arrived at Treasure Island, he had no duties to perform there; rather, he was simply awaiting transportation. He attended football games and movies and toured San Francisco. He and Marj speculated about whether or not she might be pregnant and, reading between the lines of their correspondence, it appears that it may have been their intent to accomplish that before he left for the south Pacific; however, before he left the U. S., he knew that they were not expecting a child. Indeed the couple had apparently gone so far as to discuss naming a boy "Charles" and observed that "Charles" might be getting a bit overworked as a family name.

After a wait of about three weeks at Treasure Island, CK departed for the south Pacific on October 15, 1943, on a slow Dutch transport ship. He was assigned to the Solomon Islands as a recreation non-commissioned officer until July of 1944.

Apparently his first duty station in the south Pacific was on the island of New Caledonia as he had previously written to Marj would be the case. After a few months there, he moved via the destroyer tender USS Whitney (AD-4) to the Fleet Recreation Center on Aore Island, a small island in the New Hebrides chain (now the Republic of Vanuatu).

As he wrote to Marj in one of his letters, "... my job isn't so important. Anyone could probably do it." He also reassured her that Aore was "...not far from the front but far enough to be out of danger." Indeed Aore was safe enough that First Lady Eleanor Roosevelt visited the island in September, 1943, before CK's arrival there and likewise safe enough for movie star Randolph Scott and a touring USO group to visit in January, 1944.

On Aore, CK created and maintained recreational facilities and supervised recreational activities. Troops were periodically pulled out of the fighting for a brief rest on Aore. The location featured eight baseball diamonds; football and soccer fields; volleyball, basketball, and squash courts; and a boxing ring. Presumably there were also opportunities for fishing, swimming, and lounging around. CK mentioned building barbeque pits for the sailors to use and noted that some of his petty officer peers had cooked hamburgers on ovens that he had built.

In one of his letters to Marj, CK implied that he was the senior non-commissioned officer in charge of the recreational activities on Aore and that he was the person in charge in the absence of the officer in charge. No doubt CK was a good man for whom to work. He mentioned to Marj that in contrast to most chief petty officers, he actually helped the enlisted men with the manual labor that was required such as unloading thousands of cases of beer and soda. CK also devised a system whereby the men under him got one day each week free from duty instead of having to work seven days per week. It seems clear that while CK was not in a combat situation, he did have a responsible position and that he discharged his duties very competently and creatively. In addition to his recreational responsibilities, for a while CK also had censor duty monitoring sailors' correspondence.

While CK's duties in keeping the recreational facilities operational were important to the satisfaction of Aore's clientele, in the eyes of many sailors, he also had a much more important responsibility; he was one of the non-commissioned officers who controlled the beer ration. On one occasion, CK mentioned that among his duties for the day was the unloading of ten thousand cases of beer along with a thousand cases each of Coke and Pepsi.

As CK explained the beer ration system, sailors were issued chits by their unit that could be exchanged for two beers. Often two beers were just enough to whet a sailor's thirst, and they would wind up importuning CK for more beer, offering to pay exorbitant prices for the beverage. He remarked that he could easily pocket $100 per day from selling beer outside of the chit system. That would equate to about $1480 per day in 2021 funds.

In addition to New Caledonia and Aore, CK mentioned being on Florida, and Tulagi Islands, both in the Solomon Islands chain,

Beer Chit

Ice Cream Chit

during this period, and it seems as though he had enough free time to engage with the indigenous peoples in various locations. In several letters he mentions either visits to native villages or invitations to do so, and he apparently bartered with the natives on a regular basis. He traded for a walking cane and a war club and a grass skirt for Marj. Somehow the grass skirt, said to be quite revealing, did not make it home to Marj. CK explained, apparently in response to Marj's inquiry, that he was prohibited from sending her the grass skirt.

CK was quite taken with seashells of which there was an abundance on the various islands where he was assigned. He collected seashells on Florida Island and managed to send home a fine assortment in plywood boxes that he made himself. He also made a simple tool--a can attached to a long pole--to use to retrieve shells from the clear, shallow water.

For a while CK focused his attention on collecting enough premium cat's eye shells to make his wife a necklace, but he wrote her that he was rather doubtful about his ability to do that, and apparently the project came to naught.

Shell boxes from the South Pacific

Not only did CK send home seashells, he sold them to other sailors. Apparently on one occasion he gave a native a pair of khaki pants, and the native supplied CK with shells. In April, 1944, he wrote to Marj that he had a native working for him selling shells and on several occasions that month mentioned how much money he had made. His best day apparently yielded $17, or about $250 if the $17 were converted to its 2021 value. Later that same month, CK wrote that he was giving up the shell business because too many people had stolen his idea.

CK also mentioned on at least two occasions that he had bought watches as investments. Once he wrote to Marj that he had purchased a watch for $30 and promptly sold it for $60. That would be a profit of about $440 in 2021 dollars. He also told her that he had purchased a watch that he was having repaired, presumably for resale. The remarkable aspect of this specific endeavor is that CK had connections that enabled him to find a watch repairman in the midst of a war zone.

In his correspondence CK mentioned that he sometimes brokered contacts between his native friends and associates and sailors who wanted to meet them for trade or just out of curiosity. On one occasion he made introductions for a photographer in return for photos of himself and his living area to send to Marj. Unfortunately, unlike the war club and seashell collection, those photos do not seem to have survived.

CK and Natives

April, 1944, was a memorable month for CK. Not only did he operate his shell business, he also found himself spending time in sick bay. Apparently some unknown jungle flora or fauna attacked him, and he wound up with severe swelling of his extremities and a serious rash. He acknowledged to Marj that the experience had scared him, no doubt in part because of the unknown origin of the malady.

In addition to his shell business and his military duties, he had time to build himself a bed lamp by cutting a bucket in half for a shade, to construct a small cabinet to hold his personal items, to make khaki shorts for himself, to enjoy the antics of Oscar, a pet green parrot that his group kept and for which CK built a cage, and occasionally to chase down wild chickens to supplement naval rations. Later Oscar was supplemented by a pet chicken that the sailors obtained from the local people. There was also a very small pet dog which, of course, the sailors named Peanut. CK also bartered with the native people for coconuts, bananas, limes, tangerines, oranges, and pineapples. He seems to have particularly enjoyed having pineapple to put on his ice cream when the ice cream ration came in. On one occasion CK and some of his mates used peroxide to color a group of natives' hair in return for shells.

CK lived and ate in screened-in, semi-permanent huts with access to a library, a radio, and a 1200 pound refrigerator. In his letters to Marj he commented several times that the meals were good; however, he was also very appreciative of food that people from home sent him such as candy and pecans.

Regardless of the comforts provided by his billet or the diversion generated by his duties, like most troops on overseas assignment, CK missed his wife terribly. His letters to Marj are filled with his appreciation for her reliable correspondence and with encouragement to her to continue to write faithfully. CK also implored Marj to send him photos of her on several occasions. She complied with his request, and while she did not opt for the all out Betty Grable pin-up look, there is no doubt either that CK was pleased with the result or that Marj's photos garnered her many compliments from lonely sailors.

Marj- The Pin-up Girl

CK had anticipated spending eighteen months in the south Pacific; however, in April, 1944, without telling his wife or his family, he applied to become a commissioned officer. He was selected for the navy's officer candidate school and rotated back to the United States in June, 1944, after having served about nine months in the south Pacific. His letter to Marj on June 16, 1944, makes abundantly clear his happiness about that development.

After a slow voyage home and leave time with his wife and family, he began officer's candidate school at the University of Arizona in Tucson in September, 1944. He immediately began planning to have Marj join or visit him in Tucson and fortuitously found a room to rent for her at 815 East 3rd Street. The location had the added benefit of being within easy walking distance of the area where CK's training took place. The landlord was a railroad man who probably heard stories from CK about his train conductor father-in-law as an added inducement to seal the deal.

CK's day began at 0520 and lasted until lights out at 2200. He could be out of the training area only on weekends so there was not a lot of time to spend with his wife. Still, they had just gone through a nine-month's separation, and the word was that officer candidates graduated and shipped out to their new duty station on the same day and that assignment might be overseas, so CK and Marj took advantage of every moment they could squeeze out of their time together.

In the beginning, CK expressed some concern about the difficulty of the course work; however, he successfully completed the course, whereupon he was commissioned as a lieutenant junior grade in November, 1944.

Upon completion of his officer's course, CK was assigned as the assistant recreation officer at the Mare Island Naval Base in Vallejo, California in late 1944. He served in that position until he separated from the navy in May of 1946. Marj joined him in Vallejo and worked in the safe deposit section of a bank earning $132 per month.

Lieutenant (j.g.)

In addition to a safe and easy tour of duty while stationed at Mare Island, CK and Marj also enjoyed the birth of their first child, CK Burns, Jr. This was well before the time when the sex of a child could be determined prior to birth, so CK and Marj referred to the unborn baby as "Pokey Dot." According to Marj, that name was the work of CK who was always wont to give nicknames to people. CK said that the name came from his grandmother Pocahontas and from Marj's sister Dorothy. Pocahontas was actually CK's step-grandmother, Pocahontas Maxwell Burns, the second wife of CK's grandfather, Henry Harrison Burns. CK was not her lineal descendant, but step-grandmother was probably close enough if he was simply

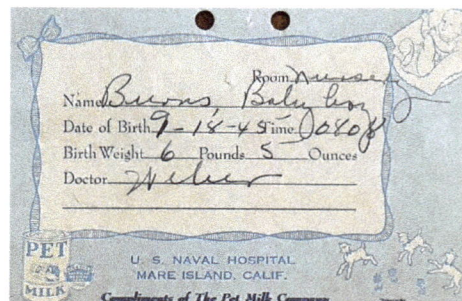

Baby Burns Card

trying after the fact to justify naming an unborn child. He also mentioned that

he was quite good at singing "Polka Dot Blues."

The birth of CK Jr. provided a bit of comic relief in that when the time

came for Marj to go to the hospital, the parents

borrowed a car from their friends Truett and

Alta Day for the trip. On the way the horn got

stuck and blared most of the way to the

hospital, no doubt announcing the imminent

arrival of CK Jr. As things turned out, CK was

not allowed to be present for the birth and had

to go outside the hospital to a pay phone to call

in and check on the progress of his son's arrival.

Truett Day and CK

Crawford

Once CK was discharged from military service, the family returned to central Texas. It may be that Marj and CK Jr., accompanied by Marj's mother, returned to Texas prior to CK, but in any event, the *Meridian Tribune* newspaper welcomed him back to Bosque County in May of 1946.

CK was attached to Valley Mills and probably would have preferred to live there and teach and coach; however, the local prohibition against both parties of a married couple teaching there was still in effect. Apparently CK saw an opportunity in Crawford which was located nine miles down the highway on the way to Temple. Living in Crawford would locate him conveniently between his mother to the west and his in-laws to the east.

CK began working in Crawford in September, 1946, as high school principal and coach. In 1947, he was chosen as superintendent. Marj taught high school math and business courses such as bookkeeping and typing.

CK, Marj, and CK Jr.

The Crawford school district was never a wealthy district because it encompassed a rural area and lacked a substantial tax base, but CK did step into a good situation in regard to physical facilities. The two-story, red brick school building had been built in 1925-26 and consisted of eleven classrooms, a laboratory, auditorium, study hall, book room, and superintendent's office. Later, in 1939, a homemaking cottage had been constructed, and in 1946, a lunchroom for 120 people was added.

Crawford School

At various times in the early twentieth century the Crawford school district had absorbed smaller adjacent districts. CK brought that process to a conclusion with the addition of the Highland and Osage districts in 1950. That action increased the size of the district to over 120 square miles.

Crawford Pirates

In the eyes of the community one of CK's most important activities was his work as coach and de facto athletic director. This was particularly true in regard to football. The school had fielded a team as far back as the 1920's, but during World War II, rationing and a shortage of male coaches had reduced the program to shambles when CK arrived in 1946.

The first football priority was to find a suitable place to play. Historically games had been played at the school on bare, hard, ground without any turf and with no seating for spectators. Fans simply drove their cars to the edge of the field and sat in them or stood by them to watch a game. Game officials were pick-ups; that is, anyone who knew a little about football and who would work for $5 per game.

Coach Burns

By the end of the 1946 season, the playing field deficiency had been remedied. The school signed a long-term lease to secure a site in Tonkawa Park that had previously been a Campfire Girls camp riding arena. Lights were erected and seating purchased. The seating consisted of surplus bomb racks obtained from the Bluebonnet Ordnance Plant in nearby McGregor for twenty-five cents per rack. As I recall the racks had either two or three levels and stood about five feet high and about six feet wide. The racks had a hole in the middle of them into which a bomb had been fitted in the rack's former life. To convert them to bleachers, the holes were covered by plywood. Happily for small children, the plywood often came undone so that a child could pop up and through the hole while playing with friends at football games.

Over the years, CK worked steadily to improve and to beautify the field. More conventional bleachers were erected as funds allowed, a concession stand and restrooms built, and a scoreboard put in place. Maintaining a beautiful turf was an on-going project. Each summer CK and school custodian Garrett "Sparky" Sparkman ran irrigation pipe from nearby Tonkawa Falls to the football field and used irrigation sprinklers to water the field during the summer months. Naturally with an abundant water supply, the grass grew tall and thick and almost always when Sparky mowed the football field he would find a few nests of baby cottontail rabbits. Ultimately Crawford came to have one of the finest fields set in one of the most scenic locations.

CK further enhanced his football program with several innovations. He pioneered the scheduling of football games on Thursday nights and persuaded the booster club to make and sell homemade ice cream at the games. Since Crawford was the only game in the area on Thursday nights, and homemade ice cream was available in a nice setting, the Pirates drew relatively large crowds including people who drove out from Waco. Seldom did the fans number more than a few hundred people but that was not bad for a town whose population was less than five hundred. Admittedly Thursday night games gave a lot of Crawford's opponents a chance to scout his team, but CK reasoned that he was going to do the same thing each year anyway so he lost nothing by letting the scouts swarm around. Conversely, he gained since new coaches in the district were always changing the approaches of his opponents, and he wanted to be free to scout them on Friday nights.

In the 1960's football scouting at the Class B high school level was not very sophisticated. The choices were to obtain the tape of an opponent's game or to send a scout to the game. CK used both techniques, and often his family was part of the process.

As time went on, CK formed a friendship with Rev. Jerry Walters, pastor of the Crawford Baptist Church and an avid Pirate football fan. Rev. Walters agreed to film games whenever there was both money to pay for filming and a sufficiently important game to be filmed. There was no money in the school or athletic budget for filming so CK persuaded the booster club to cover the cost of filming.

Normally playoff opponents agreed to exchange film. Since playoff opponents might not be known until a week prior to the game, time was of the essence in obtaining film to study. Usually tapes were sent by Greyhound Bus Lines, and they always seemed to arrive at the bus station in Waco at midnight. That meant that CK, Marj, and Debbie would all make a flying trip to Waco to pick up the film with no time lost or wasted.

Since Crawford played many games on Thursday nights, that left Friday and Saturday free for in-person scouting. Debbie and Charlie have different recollections of those scouting trips. She thinks she did more scouting than he did, while he thinks just the opposite. They do agree that the Burns family scouted as a unit, at least when the children were relatively young. CK always seemed to prefer to watch an opponent himself rather than to trust the observations of an assistant coach.

When scouting, CK had certain guidelines that he followed. The overarching principle was to have as little contact with fans of the team being scouted as possible. That meant his car was not emblazoned with Crawford decals and was not parked among those of the fans of the team being scouted. Likewise, the scouting party did not sit among the fans of the scouted team, nor did the scouts interact with those fans if at all possible. Avoiding interaction with fans was sometimes difficult since CK was well-known and recognizable in central Texas football circles, and fans would sometimes initiate conversation when they saw what he was doing or when they recognized Mr. Burns. When the scouting party left, always a little early in order to beat the crowd, assuming there were no females in the group, we would pee in the grass on the way to our car and CK would observe, "I could stand flat-footed and pee over the moon."

CK did seem to enjoy thoroughly halftime conversations with fellow coaches who were also scouting whenever he encountered them. They would frequently congregate near the concession stand and trade tall tales. Stanley Renz and E. V. Shelton from Bruceville-Eddy, Claude Everett from Valley Mills, and Clayton Oliver from Lorena were among those with whom CK preferred to interact. Mr. Shelton was grossly overweight, a fact which spurred CK habitually to refer to him as "Mr. Skelton" within the bounds of our family.

CK was not the only scout to have a set of rules to which to adhere. Debbie had a scouting agenda of her own as well. Upon arrival at a football field, her first task was to locate a restroom. When she began scouting, she was so young that this was not such a pressing issue as she could simply squat behind a car. Debbie also had to make sure that she got a trip to the concession stand prior to halftime for a Dr. Pepper and a sugary treat. The timing of the concession stand trip was crucial because Debbie wanted to watch the halftime performances in order to identify each school's colors and mascot.

Even though Debbie and CK had different objectives while scouting, CK was always aware of what was happening around him and always watched out for Debbie. On one occasion when Debbie was about six, she and CK were sitting toward the top of the bleachers while scouting the China Spring team. Debbie did a header off the top falling between the seats. As she hurtled headfirst toward the ground, suddenly she felt CK's hand around her ankle. She hung there upside down swaying back and forth while the people in the stands gasped and screamed. As CK hauled Debbie back up by her foot, the spectators burst into applause, much to Debbie's embarrassment. CK went back to scouting and making notes. CK must have felt some sympathy for Debbie since he never teased her about it. Debbie was, however, banned from the top of the bleachers for the next few scouting trips.

In regard to Crawford football, there was no such thing as a tryout. If a student wanted to play, then he went to practice, got a uniform, traveled to games, and eventually played. In the early years of the school band, some of the football players would play in the band at halftime and then rejoin the team. CK coached football, basketball, and baseball. He gave up the basketball and baseball about the time CK Jr. got to high school. Probably football was his first love, or perhaps it was simply more important in the mind of the community, so he retained control of that sport until he died. He was an excellent coach who had his system both on offense and defense, and he varied it only in the degree of complexity his personnel would let him introduce from year to year. Since in many regards Crawford played the same teams every year, other coaches knew how the Pirates would line up and what they would do. CK's team would simply execute its plan, and he would add enough variations for particular situations or in different years to keep Crawford successful. He was also a master of "gadget" or "trick" plays. Crawford was notorious for its "guard around" play. When the ball was centered to the quarterback under center, the right guard would jump into the air, execute a 180 degree turn so the he was facing his backfield, and then grab his ankle as though hurt. When the guard was in position, the quarterback would hand him the ball and then lead the backfield to the left. The guard would hesitate for a count of three and then circle around the right end. Opponents knew about this play and expected it; nevertheless, they seldom stopped it. It was much more likely that the officials, despite having been reminded of the play by

CK prior to the start of the game, would lose the ball and blow the play dead without the ball carrier being tackled.

During the period immediately prior to CK's arrival, the Crawford football program had an appalling record. The data is inconsistent in noting just how bad the Pirates were, but they were bad. One source states that during the years 1939-1945, the team won 0 games with 2 war-time seasons cancelled. Another source notes that prior to CK's arrival in 1946, the team had won only 1 game in 10 seasons. CK's first team won a district championship in 1946 and repeated in 1947.

Over 24 seasons at Crawford from 1946 through 1969, CK compiled a record of 185-58-8 for a winning percentage of .753. From 1956 through 1965 the Pirates won 10 consecutive district championships. During the 1961-1963 years the team ran off 26 consecutive wins and went undefeated for 32 games, at that time the longest undefeated streak in the state. His teams experienced only 3 losing seasons, with the most recent one occurring in 1954. It should be noted that for most of the period that he coached, Crawford was a Class B school under UIL regulations and could not compete for a state championship. The Pirates could only advance to the regional level which meant that even if they went undefeated, their season ended at twelve games. Crawford's three regional champion teams would very likely have advanced farther than a regional championship had they had the opportunity.

In recognition of his accomplishments and his contributions to the community, in 2016, the town renamed a short stretch of roadway connecting

Highway 317 with the football field as the C. K. Burns Memorial Parkway. That was a most appropriate section to select in that that stretch conjures up welcome memories for almost any former Pirate football player including the smell of cotton waste burning at the cotton gin and the lights of the field in the distance.

The school joined the town in recognizing CK's accomplishments by erecting a plaque at the football field calling attention to his achievements. I believe that these actions were brought about by the initiative of Gary Walker, a Crawford graduate, who was no doubt supported by those residents and ex-students who were old enough to remember CK and Marj during their years at Crawford.

Football Field Plaque with Jr, III, Grant and IV

I have always thought that Mr. Burns performed an important service for the town of Crawford by coaching winning teams. The town took great pride in the accomplishments of the athletic teams, and the teams fostered a sense of community spirit. This assertion was confirmed by the award of the prestigious Jinx Tucker Memorial Trophy to Crawford in 1965. The trophy is presented by the Waco Tribune-Herald newspaper in honor of a former sportswriter. The "winner of the award must exhibit overall team success, improvement throughout the season, sportsmanship, fan support and a will to win in the face of adversity." The award is open to any school, regardless of size, in the central Texas area.

Over the years I saw CK work with a number of young men who, because of their circumstances, seemed destined by their limited opportunities to regard playing football for Mr. Burns and the Crawford Pirates as one of the most memorable experiences in their lives. For those brief years that they played and won they felt a sense of worth and accomplishment that they would be hard pressed to duplicate in later life.

When I was growing up Crawford's biggest athletic rivals were Valley Mills and Midway, now known as Waco Midway. Valley Mills sat nine miles down Highway 317 from Crawford, so that rivalry was a natural one. Then too, Coach Burns had grown up in Valley Mills and probably would have worked there if he had been able to do that. He always wanted his teams to perform well when they played Valley Mills, no doubt to show the Valley what it had missed out on. In those instances when Crawford lost to the Valley, CK would acknowledge that outcome by making a trip to the winning town, frequently to get a haircut there and to greet and congratulate the Eagle fans whom he encountered. Similarly, he was diligent about attending church after a football loss, no matter how painful.

I do not know why Midway was such a rival except perhaps for the fact that CK and the Midway coach, M. T. Rice, were fierce competitors. In the early days Midway held the upper hand; however, later the tables turned and

Crawford beat Midway regularly. That was not a good experience for the larger school, and they eventually declined to play Crawford anymore.

Lady Pirates Basketball

In addition to football, CK coached most of the sports commonly offered by a Class B school including both girls' and boys' basketball and baseball. I do not recall that he coached track. He probably enjoyed his greatest coaching success outside of football in girls' basketball. His 1954 girls' team won the consolation bracket of the state tournament. That was a time when schools were not separated by size for the state tournament so that a school from the smallest classification such as Crawford, could find itself matched against a school from the largest division. Winning the consolation bracket meant that Crawford theoretically tied for the second best girls' basketball team in the state regardless of school size.

CK may have enjoyed success as a basketball coach, but he apparently found basketball to be nerve-wracking. For many years it was standard family operating procedure to play Scrabble after basketball games so that he could focus on something other than the game just completed.

School Days

In addition to being an excellent coach, CK was also an outstanding school administrator, especially working in tandem with his wife. Marj did the bookkeeping for the school and often served as a sounding board when delicate or important decisions had to be made. In the later years of their administration, it was standard practice for them to take an after-supper drive while they discussed school business secluded from the big ears of their children. I am sure that many potentially thorny issues were solved during those drives.

In the early years of their administration, a lot of on-the-job learning took place for both CK and Marj since neither had any significant experience in school administration. CK drew upon the

Admin Team

experience and counsel of County School Superintendent Joe Hatcher and of J. T. Larkin, superintendent in Valley Mills whom CK had known before the war. I have no doubt that not only administrative issues but also football was discussed with Mr. Larkin.

CK's first task was to set the Crawford school district on a firm footing. There were a number of facets to accomplishing that objective. The district profited greatly from the continuity of leadership and from the planning that Mr. and Mrs. Burns provided. CK's predecessor as superintendent, Mr. S. H.

England, served in the position for twelve years so there was a legacy of leadership upon which CK could build in moving the district forward out of the World War II era.

The success that CK and Marj had in managing the district's financial affairs went a long way toward providing a solid foundation for the district. It is probably accurate to say that the district had enough money to meet its needs but that there was little left over for discretionary items. The acquisition of non-essential items required careful planning, often with Marj poring over the budget to search for available funds here and there. Unforeseen expenses sometimes required an analogous treasure hunt before they could be satisfied.

In addition to providing steady, transparent continuity of leadership and sound, careful fiscal planning, CK helped to secure the district's future by increasing its size through the annexation of struggling, smaller districts nearby. This action provided a modest immediate increase in student population and the prospect of future development since the annexed areas were undeveloped farmland.

As the school district's finances allowed, CK oversaw the improvement of the school's physical plant. During his tenure the district added new restrooms, a gymnasium, a football field, and a baseball field.

It should be noted that one of the key elements of CK's success was the fact that he was always able to maintain the support and cooperation of his Board of Trustees, regardless of the composition of the board. This spirit of trust and cooperation meant that CK was able to administer the district rather much as he saw fit without micromanagement by the trustees. Of course, it may be that the board's supervisory approach was swayed by the delicious desserts served on special china and a designated dessert tray by CK (or more precisely by Marj) at each monthly meeting.

The strengthening of the school district was of immeasurable assistance to the community it served. As the economic life of the town wound down, residents could still remain optimistic about the future because of the strength and sense of permanence projected by the school. In many respects it was the school, primarily by means of solid academics and excellent athletics, that held the town together at a time when small-town America was dying. Later, it was primarily the quality of the school district, built in large part on the legacy of CK Burns, that drew new residents to the town and helped it to recover and to remain viable.

Probably CK's greatest contribution to both school and community was his leadership in integrating the school system in 1965. He had long demonstrated his respect for his fellow man regardless of superficial differences, and he was determined that the integration of the Crawford school district would take place in manner that afforded respect and reassurance to its African American students. I am sure that some groundwork had to be conducted among the white community; however, his children were not privy to nor witnesses of that work. Nor, probably, were most members of the community. What everyone did see was a school system that dismissed for the Christmas holidays as a segregated entity and reconvened on January 5, 1965, fully integrated without animosity or disruption. Crawford was one of the very first school districts in the state to integrate all twelve grades at one time.

One of the factors that contributed to the smooth integration of the school district was CK's empathy with the incoming African American students. He was acutely aware of their apprehension and of the likelihood that at that stressful moment they may well have preferred to have been in a different situation. He went so far as to instruct his daughter to be kind to the new students and to remind her that they would need friends at the school. He said that they would rather be at their old school with their friends than to be forced into this change. He emphasized that it was not the students who caused the situation.

CK had high expectations of himself when it came to his work as the superintendent of schools, and those expectations also extended to his family. One requirement, considered a significant burden by his children, was always to eat in the school lunchroom. The food was simply not enticing to a school-aged child. Naked wieners, concrete cornbread squares, an abundance of beans in all varieties, limp spinach, and green beans paired with hamburgers were unattractive and daunting menu items and, coupled with a distinct lack of imagination in meal planning, did not attract an enthusiastic clientele. Nevertheless, the Burns family was in the lunchroom every day for whatever offering was put forth.

There were also family guidelines about school attendance. School attendance was important because state funding depended on average daily attendance, and at Crawford, every warm body in a classroom was significant. The family sick rule was that in order to stay home from school, one had to have thrown up that morning or to have a temperature in excess of 100 degrees. Absent one of those two conditions, the puny person was expected to stagger off to school. Debbie had perfect attendance for seven years straight and ten years in all. The Burns children do not recall Marjorie ever missing school for illness, and CK was absent only on two occasions when medical conditions compelled his hospitalization.

Sometimes the various actions initiated by CK dealt with meeting, or more likely exceeding, school and community expectations of conduct. In reality the entire Burns family worked for the school, but often at no expense to the school district. As long as CK served as superintendent, Marj did the bookkeeping for the school. As far as her children know, she was never paid for that work. In addition, she performed a complex and delicate role as CK's administrative secretary, advisor, and confidant, again for no additional compensation. There is no doubt that CK valued greatly her work in these unpaid roles; however, it is equally certain that he was unwilling to risk the appearance of taking advantage of the school district by compensating her fairly.

It was important to CK to demonstrate that, like his wife, his children did not receive special or advantageous treatment. When Debbie was a ninth grader, she was elevated to the varsity basketball team by Coach Leonard Love. That was an unprecedented promotion that entitled Debbie to a varsity letter jacket; however, CK told Coach Love that Debbie did not need a letter jacket and not to order one for her. Contrary to the instructions he had received, Mr. Love put the matter to a vote by the basketball team, and Debbie received her jacket.

Charlie had a somewhat similar experience on the football team as a ninth grader. In order for the full team to scrimmage, virtually every person suited up had to participate. So, despite his small size, Charlie scrimmaged. One day early in the season the fullback, Earl Bullard, decided to have some fun at his expense. Earl was a senior who stood about 6' 2" and weighed 220. He was fast and solidly built. Conversely, Charlie was a spindly 110 pounds. On three straight plays Earl broke through the line and headed straight for Charlie, altering his course so that he could run over Charlie. Earl figured it would be great fun to run over the coach's kid. CK never suggested to Earl that he might want to cut away from a potential tackler and head for open field; he just let events play out. Perhaps it was easier for CK to remain silent because Earl never got past Charlie. Charlie tackled him every time because he was a good tackler. It looked ugly for Charlie, but Earl went down.

Similar to Marj, CK's children worked for the school in a variety of ways. During the summer, Debbie and Charlie handled the receipt of new textbooks and reallocated classroom furniture. They also helped to reposition the watering system for the football field, cleaned up after the cows who grazed on the football field, and cleaned out athletic locker rooms. They were expected to assist in cleaning up after virtually any event held at the school. CK paid his children for some of these activities, but he paid with personal funds, not with school funds. Charlie began doing janitorial work at school for fifty cents per hour; by the time Debbie was big enough to work, the rate had risen to one dollar per hour. Both children understood very clearly that they were not being given money to sit around; rather, they were expected to stay busy and to be productive.

In addition to expectations revolving around school business, there were also actions to be taken to honor and to adhere to community mores. Some of those actions were very simple and hardly remarkable, but they were emphasized nevertheless. For example, CK expected and required that his children speak to people. Neither child was enthusiastic about this activity, perhaps because they were not particularly outgoing and because they were independent and did not like to be told what to do. Charlie was especially lax about speaking to people walking up the steps to enter church on Sunday, a situation that would result in an admonition to speak to people prior to setting off for church. Charlie might or might not comply. Debbie reports being reminded to speak while walking along and then being cued by a poke in the back--a tap-speak, tap-speak, tap-speak routine.

Small Town Life

CK and Marj also adjusted their conduct to meet community expectations. The town's population was divided generally into German and non-German elements. For the most part, the Germans lived to the west of Crawford. For the non-Germans, the Germans were a somewhat exotic group. They drank beer and danced and perhaps seemed to enjoy life a bit more than the rest of the townspeople, many of whom for religious reasons, did not dance or drink. CK opted not to give offense to the religious conservatives and so neither consumed alcohol nor danced in public for many years, despite the fact that prior to settling in Crawford he had enjoyed both going dancing and drinking a cold beer occasionally. Marj reported that during this time one of CK's greatest pleasures was to go to the state basketball tournament in Austin where he (they) could drink beer and play patty-cake to his (their) hearts' content. In later years, toward the end of his life, CK and Marj amazed the Crawford community by displaying their dancing skills. It is not known if they imbibed on those occasions.

In a town as small as Crawford, everyone knew everyone else's business. The general rule was, if you did not want something known, you had better not do it. One of Marj's summer activities was to teach at United Methodist Women schools of missions. On one occasion the assigned topic was China. Among the recommended resource materials she ordered was Chairman Mao's *Little Red Book* which came to her by mail. When CK learned what Marj had done, he insisted that the book be destroyed because he wanted no gossip or criticism about her reading material. Marj complied, but she was not pleased.

The conduct of CK and Marj regarding the issues of drinking, dancing, and the *Little Red Book* are somewhat puzzling for their children at this late date. Perhaps they intended to do nothing more than to adhere to the mores of their community, but it is a bit disconcerting to find them adjusting their activities to meet the expectations of others with which they presumably did not agree.

Why Crawford?

One might wonder why, if CK was such a fantastic coach and administrator, he spent his entire post-World War II career in the tiny town of Crawford where the school never served more than about 250 students in all twelve grades and never paid him as much as ten thousand dollars in a year. Despite these disincentives, never did he seem to want to work any place other than Crawford, although in the early years remaining in Crawford was not a sure bet. In 1963, a newspaper reporter asked him why he had remained at Crawford, and CK wrote out his response. He said that

"Seventeen years ago I chose to come to Crawford as the high school coach. Perhaps influencing this decision was the fact that my wife's parents lived at Temple, my widowed mother lived in Valley Mills, and Crawford (between the two towns) seemed to be a good location. Housing, too, played a part in the decision, for it was difficult to find right after the war, and we were permitted to live with my mother in Valley Mills while teaching in Crawford.

Actually, at the time I felt that perhaps the size of the school--Class B in athletics--was a step backward for me, for I had been coaching in Class A, and just prior to the war had been elected to the coaching staff of a 4A school. I honestly felt I was qualified for a bigger school for I was a P.E. major, a college football player, and had been co-captain of a fine college team. My teammates were all stepping into fast company, and I wondered if this was the right decision for me."

CK answered the reporter's question explicitly by noting that "I receive a salary that enables my family to live in comfort and we find this a good community of active, interested, Christian people, among whom we are glad to rear our children and put down roots of living." He did also note that "had it not been for the superintendent's job, I could not have afforded to remain in a Class B coaching place." He stated that he took no additional salary for coaching.

While he did not say so explicitly, it seems likely that CK may well have felt that he owed the Crawford community a debt of sorts. At the end of World War II, when he needed a job and a chance, Crawford had given him an opportunity, and he felt like he should repay with loyal performance the chance that he had been given. When Crawford hired him, CK had never been a high school principal or school administrator, and he had only a few years of teaching and coaching experience. In essence the school district had taken a bit of a risk, and CK may have felt that he should repay the school and the town for that action--so he stayed.

Actually, unless he had been driven to perform on the stage of a larger school district, Crawford was an excellent place to work. I know of no major project or initiative that CK wanted to implement that was overruled by the Board of Trustees; rather, they trusted him and gave him free rein to administer the district as he saw fit. As Crawford's reputation prospered, he was able to choose from a large field of superior teaching applicants anytime a vacancy arose. The town took great pride in the accomplishments of the athletic teams and rightly attributed much of that athletic success to CK. After serving at World War II duty stations in Virginia, Rhode Island, the Solomon Islands, Arizona, and California, no doubt he welcomed the bucolic life he found in Crawford. In addition, he was positioned close to his mother and to his wife's parents. There was even a car furnished to the superintendent. Admittedly a 1949 Ford--later a 1951 model both with holes in the floor--may not have been much of an inducement, but it did provide basic transportation back and forth to school. Simply put, there was very little not to like about being the superintendent of schools in Crawford.

Move to Crawford

When CK and Marj began teaching in Crawford in 1946, the family resided with CK's mother in Valley Mills because there was no acceptable housing available in Crawford. Knowing CK, it would not have been acceptable to him to have resided in one place and taught in the other. Relatively quickly the family found a house to rent near the rock quarry--a place that was literally and figuratively in the wrong part of town for the superintendent of schools. Consequently, the family promptly moved when another rental house became available. This time CK and family moved near the school to what was called the "Mayberry house" from the name of the owner. We lived in the house and the owner lived next door in a garage apartment. The Mayberry house had the advantage of having space behind the house where CK was able to raise a calf named Bill along with Susie Mildred the pig.

By 1951, CK and Marj must have decided that they would become permanent residents of Crawford because they chose to build a house there.

C.K. about 1950

Marj about 1950

They purchased a vacant quarter of a block that had once been owned by either J. B. Robertson or Felix H. Robertson, both of them Confederate generals, and set about building a house. In preparation for construction, CK, his brother Dan, and additional assorted family members went to west Texas and demolished a farm building, probably a barn, to get lumber to use in building the new house. It is difficult to understand how this project could have been cost effective given that there was a lumber yard in Crawford, but had CK not thought it would be a less expensive option, he would not have done it.

The construction work was done by CK and by Jamie Damon who was one of Crawford's two professional carpenters. Eventually the two men produced a two-bedroom, one-bath, wood frame home with a garage attached by means of a breezeway. The house served CK's family very well for almost fifty years--and at a cost of $6000.

If the house was ever white like all the rest of the homes in Crawford, it was not so for very long. What I seem to remember is that while Marj was away for a few days, CK painted the house green as a surprise for her. I am sure it was a surprise when she first saw it because the green was not a soothing, gentle green; it was a brilliant Kelly green that leapt off the lot at passersby. Around the front door there was a small brown area by way of contrast, but the rest of the house was green, and so it remained until CK opted to cover the wood with imitation stone siding, Permastone. The origin of the green and brown color scheme is not known with certainty; however, presumably it arose from the fact that Marj's favorite color was green. The townspeople may have been surprised or amused by the green house, but everything worked out well in the long run. In an era before street names and numbers, the Burns family could simply direct visitors to head toward McGregor, turn right on the last street in town, and look for the green house.

New House

New House with School Car

Once the house was completed, a next order of business was to put in a garden. The Burns family always had a large garden--perhaps 120 feet by 50 or 60 feet. In the early days, the garden was plowed every spring by a team of mules, one gray and one brown. CK probably spent the most time working in the garden,

Back of House with garden

but everyone was subject to a call for labor. Frequently CK's labor calls came at times when his children preferred to play, or at least to do something other than harvest vegetables. His daughter, Debbie, was known to lure a neighbor lad, Arnold Lloyd Ramsey, into the garden where she was working, confident that Arnie would inevitably trample the plants with the result that Debbie would be instructed to take Arnie out of the garden, and thus she would escape work. The garden normally featured corn, potatoes, tomatoes, green beans, black-eyed peas, squash, cucumbers, peppers, onions, carrots, and radishes as well as other less popular vegetables.

CK enjoyed working in the garden, and he liked to be able to consume the fruits of his labor. He believed firmly that each member of the Burns family should enjoy all of the vegetables grown in the garden, not just some of them. Unfortunately, his perspective was not shared by his children who waged an on-going passive-aggressive campaign against the consumption of certain vegetables.

Gardening in Crawford, while a pleasurable past-time, was also a competitive activity. Every serious gardener strove for a plot of land that was both attractive and productive. Competition regarding tomatoes and cucumbers was particularly fierce. CK's tomatoes were respectable, but his cucumbers were exceptional, especially once Marj had processed them into her highly regarded dill pickles.

Dill Pickles

1 qt. white vinegar to 1 qt. water
1 cup salt

Place in bottom of jar —
1 grape leaf
1 garlic button
1 dill stem
1 hot pepper
Pack cucumbers and put
¼ teaspoon alum in top of jar.

3# sugar = 7 cups

Nine-Day Pickles   (sweet)

7# cucumbers soaked in salty water for 3 days-
(salty enoughtto float an egg).   Soak out in
clear water for 3 days, changing water each day.
Put in clean water to which has been added 1 pt
vinegar and 1 Tblsp alum and simmer (not boil)
2 hrs. - drain off.   Bring to a boil 3 qts.
vinegar, 3 # sugar, 2Tbls. mixed pickling spice
(tied in a bag) and our over pickles, heating
each day with spices. Can 3rd day.

Limed Sweet Pickles

(1gal)

1 C Lime (from lumber yd.) to 1 gal
water. Cover sliced cucumbers. Let
stand 24 hrs - Drain & wash. Then
put in clear water & let stand 1 hr
& let stand 1 hr - chg water doing
this every hr. for 4 hrs.
Mix { 4 c vinegar } bring to boil, add
covers to { 4 c sugar } cucumbers & simmer
5 pt { 1 tblsp spice } 45 min. Put in
{ 1 tblsp salt } jars & cover with mixture

The sense of permanency brought by the construction of the green house was augmented by the birth of CK and Marj's second child, Deborah Louise on New Year's Eve of 1952. With her birth, the family was complete.

Debbie, CK and Charlie

The Burns Family (1956)

As a part of their settling into Crawford, the mores of the time made it necessary that the Burns family find a church home. CK had grown up in the Methodist Church and Marj in the Christian Church (Disciples of Christ). In Crawford, they opted to join the Methodist Church, a choice made easier by the fact that Methodist, Baptist, or Lutheran were their only options. They were both active in their local church, and in Marj's case on a national and international scale as well. CK served on the administrative board, as Sunday school superintendent, as a trustee, as a Sunday school teacher, and as lay leader among other positions. They were faithful in attendance; despite the chagrin of their children, it was routine for the family to attend services Sunday morning and evening unless they were visiting Marj's parents in Temple. One bright spot on Sunday was the after-services noon meal. Often that featured fried chicken and mashed potatoes, or a visit to the cafe owned by Clifford and Minnie Lee Noland for a similar fried repast.

Entertainment options were limited when CK and Marj settled in Crawford. Movies were one of the few choices available to them. In fact, they had a long history of attending movies going well back into their courting days. From the letters that CK wrote to Marj, it is apparent that they went to many "picture shows" while they dated. During the war, CK encouraged Marj to go to the show, and he often took the movie boat over an adjacent island to see a show while stationed in the Solomon Islands. He especially liked westerns. When the movie theater opened in Crawford about 1951, CK and family were there for the premier presentation, *Red Stallion in the Rockies*, and remained regular attendees.

As the decade of the 1950's progressed, television became popular and began to be affordable for families. The shows were in black and white but could be enjoyed in the convenience of one's home. The first family in Crawford to get a television set was the Franklin Hodel Family. The Hodels invited 15 or 20 close friends over one Saturday night to watch *Gunsmoke* on their new television. CK liked both the experience and the western program a lot. Much to Marj's embarrassment, CK began to show up at the Hodel's back door every Saturday at 8:00 to watch *Gunsmoke*. It should be no surprise that within a few weeks, the Burns family was the proud owner of its own new television set, in part because Marj felt that it was simply unacceptable to invite yourself over for television on such a regular basis.

The first Burns television was a small black and white set that sat in the corner of the living room. It only got two channels, 6 (Temple) and 10 (Waco). Each TV needed an antenna on the roof for reception. Early TV's had an interesting quality of rolling. The picture would roll and roll until you jiggled the controls. There was no remote – your children were the remotes. The children fixed the roll, switched channels and fetched snacks. Over the years, Debbie developed a special talent for stopping the roll. CK convinced Debbie it was an important job, and she took it seriously. Debbie took after CK and was more enamored with television than her brother, Charlie. When she was small, Debbie spent many hours sitting in CK's lap in his big chair watching television. Later, she graduated to lying on the floor so she could jump up and reach the controls quicker.

CK's favorite shows were *Gunsmoke, Wagon Train, Rawhide* and *Bonanza.* The family had to leave Temple by 7:00 PM on Sunday nights after visiting Marj's parents so that they would be home by 8:00 for *Bonanza.* During football season, CK often spent Saturday and Sunday watching football games with his play book beside him drawing up plays.

In the 1960's, color television became affordable for families. The LeRoy Mappe family invited CK, Marj, and Debbie over to watch their new color TV. When the NBC peacock spread his colorful feathers, Debbie and CK were smitten. As soon as they got in the car, Debbie wanted to know when they could get a color television.

While no doubt Marj appreciated the entertainment value of color television, she also thought that a color set was simply too expensive, so, Debbie and CK tried another approach. What if they saved the money to buy a color set? Marj agreed if they saved the money then they could get a color TV. Thus, began the "Great Quarter Saving Campaign". For months, Debbie collected every quarter that came into the house. Eventually, victory was declared. Marj, CK and Debbie went to Lammert's Appliance Store in McGregor to pick out a color television. They came home with a Spanish style combined color TV, radio and stereo record player that required at least 2 men to lift. They also purchased two new antennas, one small and one large. The antennas added Dallas stations. The additional antennas sometimes required a climb on the roof to change the alignment of the antenna, a new job for children (mostly Charlie). CK and Debbie were thrilled the night when the NBC peacock spread his colorful feathers in their very own living room. The TV console lasted until Marj moved out of the house many years later.

As noted above, Marj traveled both nationally and internationally on behalf of various entities of the Methodist Church; however, other than those travels, the family did not venture far from Crawford. In part, the failure to travel much may have stemmed from the fact that CK worked the year round as superintendent. During the school year normally only the custodian arrived at work before CK, and in the summer, CK usually worked every morning at school.

Fishing

Summer afternoons were often set aside for fishing, usually in Hog Creek or the North Bosque River at Valley Mills. Probably these were places at which CK had fished all his life--his early letters to Marjorie indicate that even then he was a dedicated fisherman. He was also a serious fisherman. There were those in Crawford who wanted to accompany him fishing, but in order to become a repeat fishing companion, they had to adhere to CK's unspoken rules of fishing conduct. Among other things, they could not be loud or disturb the water where they were fishing, they could not engage in unnecessary conversation while fishing, and they could not fish too close to where CK was fishing. If they failed to follow these guidelines, they were not likely to be invited again. Unfortunately, despite numerous opportunities to do so, neither Marj nor CK Jr. enjoyed fishing. Debbie, however, became a stalwart fishing companion.

In the summer, CK would come home from school and tell Debbie that it was time to go catch grasshoppers for bait. They would load their glass jars in the car and head for Sparky's pasture located a couple of miles out of town on Highway 317. Occasionally Charlie or the Ramsey boys who lived next door would be shanghaied for the bait detail.

Once the bait party was in the pasture, bottles were distributed, and everyone took off running after yellow grasshoppers. No other color or kind would do. Everyone would keep catching until CK called a halt. Then it was back to the house to release the bait crew and to prepare the fisherpersons' lunch of choice: Dr. Pepper, saltine crackers, and Vienna sausages.

CK had various fishing locations. He rarely fished from a boat. At least once a year the family would go to Marble Falls and stay at "The Ramp" which was a small collection of non-descript cabins located just below Max Starcke Dam in Marble Falls. CK especially liked to fish at night when the dam was generating. Marj mostly stayed in the air-conditioned cabin while Charlie wandered around. CK, however, would look at the lights of Marble Falls and remark to Debbie that he would not mind retiring next to the river so he could fish more.

Another occasional fishing location, usually set aside for the cooler part of the year, was a barge on Lake Belton. When Debbie was too young to fish, Charlie would go with CK to the barge. He could read a book while CK fished, and if things got too slow, he would go to the car and sleep. When Debbie became able to make the barge trips, CK would schedule one for a time when Marj was out of town on church work. He would assemble a quartet of fisherpersons that included his friends Bill and Willie Mattlage, and they would go for a night on the barge. The barge was well-equipped with a snack bar, lights, and heaters. Fishermen could drop a line through holes in the floor or stand at the edge of the barge and cast out into the lake. The one amenity the barge lacked was en suite restrooms. There were two old outhouses on the shore. In practice, that meant dashing across the boardwalk to shore, scrambling up to the parking lot, taking a deep breath and flinging open the door. Without inhaling, one did one's business, and then burst free to gulp fresh air. Willie was tasked with keeping an eye on Debbie during toilet runs in the wee hours of the night.

There was a spot on Hog Creek between Crawford and Valley Mills that was probably CK's favorite fishing hole. CK knew the landowner and could always finagle permission to fish there. It didn't hurt that CK gifted the man with a carton of cigarettes from time to time.

The location on Hog Creek was a great place to fish. It had both deep water and shallow water along with plenty of minnows to seine for bait. CK taught Debbie to seine, but that was a struggle for her since he was 6' 3" and she was not. It was not unusual for Debbie to go under water and then come up only to hear "Keep the seine down. Keep it down" The best feature of the Hog Creek location was that it had shallow places where Debbie could play without infringing on CK's fishing territory and still allow her to be close enough to answer quickly a call for additional hands.

Debbie and CK spent a lot of time together fishing. He taught her to sing several songs, bait a hook, clean a fish, catch grasshoppers for bait, and fish. They always ended a fishing trip singing "You Are My Sunshine" on the way home. CK would say to Debbie that she was the best daughter in the world and she would tell him that he was the best daddy in the world.

CK told Debbie that when he retired, he wanted to be close to a creek or body of water so that he could fish.

For CK fishing was not only about sport or pleasure; there was a utilitarian purpose as well. Every Fourth of July CK hosted a family fish fry at his house. The attendees included his brothers, cousins, and nieces and nephews as they got older. In CK's mind, the goal was to host a catfish fry, and he was disheartened on those few occasions when his fishing efforts did not result in a sufficient number of catfish, and he was forced to supplement the menu with crappie or bass. The family bought a freezer in which to store the fish. When fish were caught, they were cleaned and placed in gallon wax milk cartons filled with water and frozen. CK made careful calculations of the number of fish on hand compared to the number of guests expected. The closer July 4th came, the more frequent the inventories of fish. Only one year did CK fall short and have to purchase fish, something that was not revealed to the attendees. The annual fish fry was also a time when CK could display his gardening prowess since the menu usually included fresh vegetables from the garden. Frequently the guests went away laden with garden produce. It is my recollection that CK and Marj did virtually all the cooking for this annual gathering. CK would fry the fish in large black kettles while his brothers and cousins stood around kibbitzing, and Marj would prepare the rest of the food. She would be sure to see that there was plenty of Burns tea and an abundance of desserts, including Grandma's chocolate pie, both tea and desserts saturated with sugar.

Grandma's Chocolate Pie

Since the subject of food has arisen, we should probably take a moment to explore that topic in greater detail. Succinctly put, the Burns cuisine was constructed on sugar and grease, as was typical of CK's era. Those who married into the family were graciously extended some leeway regarding their eating preferences; however, a Burns by blood always displayed a marked affinity for sugary foods, especially desserts. At reunions and family gatherings there would be a table for meats, for vegetables, for breads, for numerous pitchers of insanely sweet iced tea, and several tables--yes, multiple tables groaning under the weight of bountiful desserts. The shining star of the desserts, at least in the opinion of CK and his children, was Grandma Celia's chocolate pie. Indeed, the grandchildren were so enamored of that pie that they perfected a technique to jump the serving line and get their desserts first before moving on to less exciting foods.

By the time that Debbie was old enough to appreciate the chocolate pie, the recipe had passed from Celia to Marj, no doubt because the chocolate pie was one of CK's favorite foods. Marj did not enjoy the pie to the extent that her family did, but her role as the baker was crucial.

Each pie was shared, ostensibly equally, among CK, Charlie, and Debbie. The pie did not last long. CK and Charlie ate their portions very quickly, while Debbie was more deliberate in order to prolong the pleasure. Everyone had a unique approach to eating the pie. Debbie isolated the chocolate filling, the most desirable part of the pie, by first flipping the slice of pie over to dispose of the crust and then consuming the meringue. Charlie ate the back crust first and then enjoyed the filling and the meringue together. CK simply devoured his share.

Sharing the pie went fairly smoothly and equitably until the time when Charlie left home. Once he left, Debbie eagerly anticipated having a full half of a pie all to herself. She looked forward to spreading out consumption of her treasure over several days. As the pie eating progressed, Debbie noted that she did not receive a whole half of the pie. She discussed this disparity with CK whose response was that he had not understood that the pie was to be strictly divided in halves. That satisfied Debbie, and she regarded the matter as resolved.

The next time a pie was baked, Debbie cut the pie into two halves to remind CK of the pie-sharing protocol. She envisioned savoring her half of the pie over several days. However, as things developed, the pie did not last that long due to violations of the sharing rule. Debbie saw that both halves of the pie were decreasing, and she knew that that decrease was not attributable to her. She confronted CK who observed that he was unsure which half was his so he just ate from the larger side. In Debbie's view, he had simply been eating off both halves.

Debbie solved the equity issue with the next pie. Once again, she cut the pie in half, but this time she stuck toothpicks in her half to mark it. That allowed her to prolong the enjoyment of her pie; however, she did have to deal with comments from CK such as "your ole' Dad sure does wish he had some chocolate pie." Debbie was able to stay strong and safeguard her pie when she recalled the whistling incident.

Grandma's Chocolate Pie Recipe

Ingredients:

  1 heaping cup of sugar

  4 tablespoons of flour

  3 tablespoons of cocoa

  1 teaspoon of vanilla

  1 1/2 cups of milk

  3 egg yolks well beaten

  2 tablespoons of butter

Directions:

  Mix sugar, flour, and cocoa

  Add vanilla, milk, egg yolks, and butter

  Cook in double boiler until thick

  Pour into pie crust, top with meringue from egg whites

Vacations

When the family did take vacations, they were sometimes tied to fishing as were the periodic trips to Marble Falls, but on other occasions the family acted more like conventional tourists. Generally, the trips were made by car within the state of Texas. Austin and San Antonio were frequent destinations for historical attractions. The family on occasion visited Houston for a combination vacation and football coaching school.

There were a few certainties about Burns family vacations. It was a given that food would be taken from home to be eaten at a roadside park in route to the destination. There was also an unwritten rule that the family would lodge at a tourist court (as they were called then) that featured a swimming pool. Presumably, the swimming pool was for the benefit of family members other than CK since I do not remember him ever swimming while on vacation. Likewise, CK seems to have been ambivalent about the vacation destination and about vacation activities. My guess is that CK would have been more content fishing for a week rather than taking a vacation; he took short trips to nearby destinations in order to humor his family.

Later in life there were some longer vacation trips, sometimes taken together with another couple, Shorty and Leroy Mappe. One such trip was the Arkansas Caddo burial trip. That journey began with a letter. Shorty Mappe happened to mention that she had gotten an advertisement about vacation cabins in Arkansas with fishing. With the word "fishing" CK's ears perked up.

Shorty brought out the pamphlet which showed nice cabins, a river out the back door and a miniature golf course on the cabin property. Needless to say with fishing and miniature golf on the table, Debbie and CK were sold. Thus, it was decided, the summer vacation destination would be Arkansas.

When summer rolled around, the vacation participants were CK, Marj, Shorty, Leroy and Debbie who was 13. Charlie did not go because he was working. The Mappe children were grown and gone. The vacationers loaded up the Mappe's car and took off for central Arkansas.

The group arrived only to discover that the camp was not quite as expected. Debbie remembers looking at Shorty and Marj's expressions and knew that the cabins did not live up to their expectations. The river was out the back of the cabins, but it was a raging, cold river with no banks from which to fish. The miniature golf course was there, but it was cement.

The fishermen tried fishing the next day but quickly returned to the cabin reporting that the water was too cold and too swift. No fish could catch the bait as it was swept downstream. The fishermen were expected to wade in the water to fly fish. The fishing equipment was returned to the car with great sadness.

Since fishing was no longer available, the group became day trippers. They went on a day trip to Hot Springs. Debbie pointed out that there were lots of billboards for the Caddo burial grounds and for "find a diamond" locations. The adults began teasing Debbie about the Caddo burial grounds and the "find a diamond" opportunities every time they saw a billboard, so much so that Debbie quit talking about it.

During the day trips, Shorty and Marj admired the pine trees. They convinced their husbands to pull over on the side of the road and dig up small pine trees to take home with them. Debbie remembers thinking that they were going to get arrested. She also wondered why these pine trees would flourish when no pine trees grew in Crawford?

CK soon took pity on Debbie and organized a miniature golf game one night. They all played on the unlevel cement with the teenage boy who lived on site supervising, leading to more comments for Debbie. That, along with the Caddo burial grounds teasing, made Debbie envious of Charlie at home.

On one of the driving excursions, the group began to see Caddo burial signs ahead, which of course, started the teasing again. When the group got to the entrance, CK told Leroy to turn in. He said that he and Debbie were going to see the burial grounds. Everyone else chose to sit in the car.

When CK and Debbie got inside, he told her to take her time that the others could just sit in the car. Debbie was thrilled. CK also told her that she did not need to get the people in the car a souvenir.

Thus, the first non-family or football-related trip ended. It wasn't a complete failure. Marj and Shorty got their pine trees, which soon died, Debbie got to see the Caddo burial grounds and returned loaded up with Caddo burial ground souvenirs. She also came back with an appreciation of her Dad who teased her but loved her enough to visit the Caddo burial grounds.

An Exemplary Life

CK Burns came from humble beginnings to make a significant impact on the town in which he lived and on the many students that he taught--whether the lessons came in the classroom or on the athletic field. Much of his influence came from the fact that he was a formidable, honorable, and respectful man. He could be a force, a presence, although generally he worked quietly and unobtrusively.

Part of CK's formidable aura stemmed from his physical attributes. As noted earlier, he was a big man, even by current standards, and all the more so in his day. He was also a superb athlete even into middle age. I recall an incident that occurred when he was about forty-five years old. One of his brother Wallace's sons was being rude and mouthy to his father in CK's presence. Wallace did nothing, but CK soon had enough of the boy's impudent behavior. Without warning, CK grabbed his nephew by the biceps, swung him into the air until the boy was upside down, and then slowly lowered him to the ground headfirst. CK concluded the exercise by instructing the boy to get in his car and be quiet. Needless to say, there was stunned compliance.

Much more at play in creating a formidable aura was CK's command presence. This may have arisen from his leadership roles on athletic teams and from his naval service during which he spent extended periods of time training sailors. Whether dealing with school students or with his adult peers, he very seldom had to raise his voice; rather, he simply spoke and people listened.

Several of the situations related earlier illustrate CK's finely-honed sense of honor and integrity. He was determined that his actions and those of his family would always reflect favorably on the Crawford school system and on the community in general. He understood and accepted the notion that he was in many ways an ambassador for the school and the town. His sense of honor and his understanding of his representational role came to the fore in his coaching conduct. I cannot recall a single instance when he protested an official's call or when he became embroiled in a dispute with a rival coach--nor did he criticize officials or coaching peers after the fact. A few notable illustrations of this conduct come to mind. In 1959, Crawford played Dawson for a football regional championship. The game was close and hard-fought. As time was running out, Dawson led by two points, but Crawford was about to score the winning touchdown. The referee marked the ball ready for play which started the clock. Then he failed to get out of the way promptly so that Crawford could run a play before time ran out. Simultaneous with the expiration of time, Crawford scored--but too late. The referee's conduct had been clear for fans to see, and Crawford fans were livid. CK said not one word of complaint or criticism because that was simply not the way he conducted himself. I am, however, quite confident that he took no small pleasure in beating Dawson 62-0 for a regional championship in 1961.

A few seasons later Crawford was matched against a woebegone Axtell Longhorn team. The Crawford team was very good, so good that Axtell could not prevent them from scoring. Soon the score mounted to a level that CK could not in good conscience justify exceeding. He instructed his team that when Axtell ran out of downs and had to punt the ball, to punt the ball back to them during that same play thus preventing an offensive possession by Crawford and a further increase in the score. While the final score was something like 70-12, it would have been much worse had CK not shown respect for the Axtell team and exercised a large portion of mercy.

In 1967, the normally hapless Bruceville-Eddy Eagles rose up and smote their foes to claim a district championship. The icing on their cake was a victory over Crawford on Crawford's Homecoming. The Waco newspaper reported that it was the first victory ever for Bruceville-Eddy over Crawford. Strictly speaking that may not have been true, but it certainly was the first victory in recent memory. While the loss must have been galling to CK, he appreciated what the Eagles and their coach and his friend Clayton Oliver had accomplished. Not only did CK appreciate Bruceville-Eddy's achievement, he recognized it publicly by taking the unprecedented action of sending the Crawford school band to Bruceville-Eddy's bi-district game to support them.

CK showed respect not only to opposing athletic teams but also to the members of his community and to his family. Periodically the African-American church in Crawford would need to "borrow" a school bus in order to make a trip out of town. In order to do that, they would need to speak to CK.

My recollection is that a couple of church members would visit our house on Sunday afternoon during the summer. I would answer the door and invite them in. They would politely decline and remain standing outside in the heat. When CK appeared, he would insist that they come inside and sit in the air conditioned comfort of our living room to discuss their request. As far as I know, their request to use a school bus was never declined.

In the early 1960's, well before the Stonewall Riots and the beginning of the exercise of gay rights, CK also extended respect to a member of the gay community--at least superficial appearances indicated that the gentleman was gay, to wit: the gentleman was a stylish and fastidious dresser, and he had a steady male "friend" with whom he resided. The man was clearly out of the ordinary for Crawford, both for the school and the community. Notwithstanding what appeared to be a questionable fit with a rural environment, CK hired the man as high school principal, and events ran smoothly until the man decided voluntarily to move on to another position.

Perhaps it was financial difficulties in his birth family or just a good heart, but CK was always generous to those who were financially less fortunate than was he. Louis Reese and Leonard Simpson were frequent beneficiaries of CK's kindness. Louis lived in Crawford, and Leonard lived about five miles outside of town on the way to Valley Mills. Neither man had access to a vehicle so they traveled on foot. Traveling by foot in central Texas in the summer months was hot, sweaty, dirty business. CK never failed to offer these men a ride if he had room in the car--and he taught his son to do the same thing.

CK also provided an example of respect and kindness in dealing with one of his elementary students. After he was diagnosed with a stomach ulcer, CK drank milk every morning after he arrived at school. He would send me to the lunchroom to get two cartons of milk out of the refrigerator. Then he would call Sammy, an elementary student, down to his office to share a carton of milk. Sammy was dropped off early for school, and CK either knew or surmised that Sammy got little for breakfast each morning. He knew that Sammy qualified for a free lunch, but he also understood that it was a long time from waking up to lunch time and that Sammy would be hungry.

CK was also thoughtful and considerate regarding the treatment of the members of his family. In an era when it was generally accepted that father really did know best, CK and Marj generally made important decisions as equals without one deferring habitually to the other (notwithstanding the affair of Chairman Mao's *Little Red Book*). In addition, CK supported his wife in her church work which included travel and stays away from home by herself at a time when such things were not routinely done by women. CK and Marj respected their children by allowing them the freedom to exercise judgment and to make their own choices.

The Private Side

There are some additional things that one should know about CK in order to understand him more fully. I would say that his public persona was quiet and reserved, perhaps in part because of his self-imposed code of conduct as a representative of school and community, but he could be absolutely charming when circumstances indicated such a role for him. Among family and close friends, he displayed a wicked sense of humor and an ability to lie skillfully and convincingly in pursuit of merriment. Frequently he bestowed nicknames he had made up on people and places. His brother Wallace was first known as "Son" and later as "Wad." Wad's oldest child, Lou Ann, was referred to as "Stinky" while her brother Danny was designated as "Hillbilly. CK's uncle, Clarice Clemons was known as "Clabber." Anyone who was caught doing something which was suspect in CK's eyes was immediately called to task as "Rusty," probably a shortened version of "Rusty Butt." Both his daughter and his daughter-in-law were known as "Bright Eyes," and his "Pokey Dot" son has already been mentioned.

In order to be a Burns, you had to be able to take a joke and preferably to be able to make a joke as well. There was a level of kidding for the outside world, and then there was the Burns level of kidding. Humor, even of a rough and ready variety, was important to CK. In his early letters to Marj, he tells her how much he likes her because she can take a joke. Later, when CK was away in the navy, his mother wrote to him that Marj was a true Burns because she could "kid." Of course, there are a few letters to Marj in which CK has to explain to her that he was just kidding about something and did not mean to upset her.

When CK kidded with his brothers and his relatives like his cousin Jake Bonds, everyone understood that the game was on, but that also meant that something was missing--an unsuspecting straight man. Ultimately that missing piece was supplied by CK's daughter Debbie. She was the perfect straight man because she adored her dad and believed everything that he told her. CK's son Charlie became his assistant and gleefully participated in CK's jokes.

For example, at a summer lunch, CK's approach to Debbie might go something like this: "Were those plums on the table? Yes, of course. Aren't those your favorites? Why would you think that they were cherry tomatoes? What? Of course those are mashed potatoes. No, we would never give you mashed turnips. We know you don't like mashed turnips."

Occasionally CK's work with his straight man went off the tracks. When the family was in the car and someone farted, CK and Debbie would sing out, "someone tooted" and then begin to assign blame. Once, on a Sunday afternoon drive with friends, someone passed a bit of silent, deadly gas, whereupon Debbie shouted out, "someone tooted," causing an awkward moment of silence since the offending party was not a family member. Later CK had to explain that some jokes were only for the family.

By far the most elaborate joke with his straight man daughter was "the whistler." When Debbie was about five years old, she wanted desperately to learn how to whistle. CK told her he would teach her. He told her to purse her lips and blow which she did. Then she started to hum "who, who, who" in the tune of a song. CK told her she was a wonderful whistler. Charlie confirmed her talent and both he and CK requested songs for her to whistle. Debbie was especially good at "California, Here I Come." Marj did not ask for any special songs, but neither did she tell Debbie that she wasn't really whistling.

Debbie's whistling went on for several weeks until her friend Arleen Hawkins came home with her one Sunday after church. Debbie decided to impress Arleen with a surprise rendition of "California, Here I Come;" however, Arleen informed Debbie that she was not whistling. Debbie countered that she was whistling, and the disagreement escalated until an outraged Debbie announced that she would prove she was whistling. With Arleen in tow, Debbie marched into the house and threw open the door to the bedroom where CK and Marj were napping.

Debbie stepped up to Marj for support and said, "Mama, tell Arleen that I am whistling!"

With a sheepish look on her face, Marj replied, "Well, no, Debbie actually you are not."

During this exchange CK was lying in bed with a horrified look on his face because Debbie had brought Arleen into his bedroom during his nap and because "the whistler" joke had backfired so spectacularly.

Debbie left the room furious at having been played as a straight man. The joke, however, has followed her for fifty plus years; she still receives requests to whistle special songs from family members.

The following day CK installed a lock on his bedroom door.

"Sookie"

As we conclude this narrative, we would like to include a series of incidents and anecdotes that we his children recall that help to illustrate CK's character and personality.

One of my very early memories is of being carried from the car into our house by CK at night. When I was little and sleepy I would lay my head on his shoulder, and he would softly say to me, "Bud, I 'preciate you." He was not all that big on saying that he loved me, but I got a lot of "I 'preciate you's".

When both of his children were small, they would ask him to tell them stories at night, and he would readily oblige since making up tall tales was an easy thing for him to do. I recall that her father told Debbie stories about Ham and Eggs who were two mice brothers. Decades later I took those two characters and created a new set of stories about their adventures. I always wanted to hear stories about when CK was in the war--in the navy. He would respond with a recounting of the single Japanese bomber that would make a brief attack during the nightly movie causing everyone to abandon the movie for the relative safety of a slit trench. When the bombing was over, the movie would resume.

We are uncertain of the origin of CK's "Sookie" nickname. Our best guess is that it was a corruption of "CK" which his niece or nephew could not pronounce. Over several decades I heard his niece Lou Ann use it frequently and comfortably enough to think that it might well have originated with her; however, when asked, she claimed to have no knowledge of either the nickname or its origin. Apparently CK carried it with him to North Texas where Marj's cousin, Mildred Cabiness Goldthwaite picked it up. Likewise, CK's lifelong friends Truett and Alta Day used it during their time together in the navy.

When I was just old enough to remember the event, CK participated in a womanless wedding. The affair took place in February, 1950, for the benefit of the Crawford PTA. For an admission cost of $.55 one could enjoy both a fashion show and a wedding with all the participants local men in drag. CK had a starring role as the bride. In a deliberate mismatch, he towered over the groom. As it was later told to me, one of the few snags was finding a suitable dress large enough for CK; there were not a lot of women who were prepared to acknowledge that their clothes would fit a person of CK's size. Apparently, such performances were successful enough to warrant repetition since there are photos of CK as both a bride and a flower girl.

CK as a flower girl

Given CK's athletic abilities, it would have been difficult to have equaled or to have exceeded his sports accomplishments. He never put any pressure on me to perform well or even to participate; nevertheless, I wanted to make him proud somehow. Football was my best option, and I turned out to be good enough to earn his respect. However, I lacked the size and speed to play beyond high school. In contrast to post-high school athletic accomplishments, of which there would be none, CK recognized my academic endeavors and carried a copy of my college grades with him to show people when they inquired about my activities.

Despite the fact that CK wanted his children to do well academically and athletically, he was never known to yell at them from the sidelines or the stands--neither to praise or to encourage them nor to criticize them. Our guess is that he simply thought that such behavior would have been unseemly. He did work with his children at home to improve their skills, and infrequently at home he might have a quiet word with them about some aspect of their performance, but he never exhorted them publicly.

That is not to say that CK failed to work with his children to improve their athletic performance although his approach with them varied. As a young boy Charlie caught hundreds if not thousands of passes thrown by CK. In retrospect, one can surmise that CK may have wanted to make Charlie an end as he had been. Charlie could catch the ball if he could see it, but looking out of a sweaty football helmet through steamed glasses under dark lights was hardly a recipe for success, and he was soon converted to another position.

When Charlie was a senior, he played defensive end. One of his responsibilities was to ensure that no opposing runner got outside of him and turned the corner up field. Charlie was very good and no one got around him until the China Spring game. Then, on two occasions, Charlie was beaten. CK did not admonish Charlie, but rather simply called him over to the sideline and out of anyone's hearing quietly asked him what was wrong. Charlie responded that his left leg hurt. With no further ado, Charlie was dispatched to the doctor the following Monday to have a large hematoma drained.

Debbie had a somewhat different experience with CK's coaching. Debbie never remembers CK telling her what to do during a basketball game; however, once she made varsity, he would coach her at home after a game in private coaching lessons. CK would have Marj play defense. Let us just say that Marj had never played basketball in her life but was an extremely energetic and willing participant in the coaching sessions. Marj would throw her arms in the air, wave them up and down and run back and forth in front of Debbie. In the first session, Marj's technique stunned both CK and Debbie. Once they stopped laughing and got the defense under control, CK showed Debbie some ways to get around a defensive player. These coaching sessions became a regular occurrence after the games. Debbie missed these sessions very much after CK died.

Mention has already been made of the townspeople's surprise when they learned that CK could dance and drink beer. Not only were the townspeople astounded, so were his children. In fact, his children did not know that he enjoyed a cold beer until well after his death. Apparently that information was simply not something he felt his children needed to know. Indeed, the knowledge that CK liked an occasional beer freed his son to indulge as well, something that had not previously been the case.

CK always wanted his wife to look nice, and he greatly enjoyed helping her do that. It was customary for him to present her with clothes on any holiday or special occasion. As I recall he preferred that his selections display a bit of flash and color so that Marj would stand out in a room full of people. He had a good eye for color and knew just what would work to set Marj off without at the same time overwhelming her peers. He was always very pleased when one of his selections worked out well.

In CK's world view, the only way to be on time was to be early. When there was family travel involved, CK would back the car out of the garage and sit and wait for the rest of the family. After time passed, he would become impatient and honk the horn. The honking would infuriate Marj since she operated on a different view of punctuality. In addition, when Marj was left overseeing the dressing of her younger child, she did not appreciate being hurried without also being helped.

CK never minded spending money to dress his wife, but in many other areas he could be quite frugal. A family watchword attributed to CK was "Don't buy it, I'll build it." Of course not everything could be built, but there were some notable attempts. When I needed a set of weights to use in preparing for football, CK made them. He poured concrete in coffee cans and inserted a bar. The homemade weights were perfectly serviceable; however, the heavier of the two sets that he made only weighed about thirty-five pounds with the result that I had to do dozens of repetitions in order to benefit. On another occasion Marj wanted a desk at which she could work. No doubt she envisioned a nice piece of furniture that would be suitable for the master bedroom. What CK constructed for her was a piece of plywood laid on top of two, two-drawer filing cabinet drawers. To top things off, CK painted his creation a pale green. Marj was not pleased, but soon after a third bedroom was added to the house, and the desk was left behind.

As a reader may have noticed, CK had an appreciation of money and of the work that was required to earn money. Drawing upon his connections, CK was able to turn up a number of jobs for his son. Some of these jobs turned out nicely such as hauling hay for a local dairy farmer and unloading trucks on a freight dock. Others, like loading turkeys on a tractor trailer truck and mowing a neighbor's large yard for a pittance, did not work out nearly so well from his son's point of view (or of his daughter who inherited chores when her brother moved on). Conversely, CK seemed interested more in the fact that there was money to be made, without undue concern for the nature of the task.

CK was willing to help his neighbors utilizing his children to do the work. For instance, he set the price for neighboring widows at $2.00 for his daughter to mow their very large yards with deep roadside ditches.

CK took great pride in his home and strove diligently to see that it was always maintained appropriately. That meant that the yard had to be maintained to CK's standards--and there were procedures for doing that. For example when mowing, the cut grass was always to be thrown on to the uncut area so that when the job was completed, there would be no unsightly cut grass residue lying about. CK was also particular about trimming around the house and trees. Before I was old enough to mow, I was assigned the task of trimming using a pair of kitchen scissors. As I recall, it took a very long time to work all the way around the house wielding a pair of dull kitchen shears.

I never knew the origin of his desire, but CK always indicated that he wanted to keep a few farm animals. There would have been no room to do that at the green house, but CK did keep a pig and a calf when the family resided in the Mayberry house. Later in life CK would occasionally mention his desire to buy a few acres of land on which he could maintain a few head of cattle. I have always thought it was a tragedy that he never got to fulfill this modest wish.

There are photos of CK wearing short pants during his World War II service in the south Pacific, and he wrote about making shorts to wear there; however, except when he was fishing, I never knew him to wear shorts in later years, no matter how hot the day or the nature of the task at hand. Apparently, men of his era simply did not do that.

CK had a number of nieces and nephews in which he took an active interest. His brother Wallace produced the first niece and nephew whom CK promptly tagged as Stinky and Hillbilly. Wallace's third child was Charles Oscar Burns, but since CK also had a son named Charles, presumably he declined to yield that name to his nephew with the result that Charles Oscar became Oscar in CK's terminology. Notwithstanding the name issue, CK habitually invited his nephews Oscar and Mike to spend time with his family during the summer, an activity which they both seemed to enjoy.

CK also hosted his wife's nieces and nephews. One of the highlights of Debbie's summer occurred when her Miller cousins came to visit Grandmother

Jones in Temple. The cousins lived in Albuquerque, New Mexico and came for two to three weeks. There were twin boys, Rick and Bob, who were three years older than Debbie, and a girl, Barb, who was Debbie's age. They were quite exciting to Debbie because they said things like "you guys" instead of "ya'll," they lived in a city spelled with not one but two "q"s, and worst of all, they lived in a state without Dr. Pepper.

Usually, Debbie would go to Temple to stay with them for a week. Sometimes when driving to Temple, CK would tell Debbie to lie down in the back seat and sleep so the trip would go faster. Once Debbie started to drift off to sleep, CK would begin to wave, honk the horn, and say, "Why hello Bob, Rick, Barb! So glad to see you!" Debbie would jump up looking for her cousins only to find that the car was still a long way from Temple.

Sometimes the cousins would come to Crawford to stay a few days with Debbie. During one of these visits, CK decided to help Marj entertain the extra kids. CK lined up all the kids and told them they were in the army. CK was the commander, and the kids were all privates. He said that if they worked hard, they could earn promotions. He told them that he was in charge of promotions.

CK was quite pleased with the early performance of his troops. He had kids running here and there doing all sorts of chores. Mowed and trimmed the yard--promotion! Pulled up the dead cornstalks from the garden--another promotion! Moved furniture at school--promoted again! Assisted in watering the football field--more points toward promotion!

Things went so well that CK offered his troops some rest and recreation in the form of a swimming and fishing expedition to the North Bosque River at Valley Mills. The commander felt that he had his troops well in hand and did not need assistance with the undertaking.

Unfortunately, his troops did not comprehend that there were certain rules and procedures to be followed while fishing. For example, no swimming or fishing was allowed in the immediate area where the commander was fishing, nor were loud noises allowed there. Troops were not allowed to handle the tackle box or its contents, even if it was open and the contents tantalizingly available.

Despite Debbie's efforts to explain both the rules and the consequences of failing to adhere to them, her Miller cousins did not understand the situation. Disaster was inevitable. It came when cousin Bob opened the tackle box, removed a lure, tied the lure to his line, and tossed his line into the water where CK had been fishing. CK immediately adopted his best command presence and ordered everyone to pack up and to load the car for the drive home.

Once CK and his crew returned to Crawford, he busted them all back to the rank of private E-1 with no hope of promotion and ended the army game for the duration on the visit.

Despite this unfortunate outcome, apparently all was not lost. Here is what Bob Miller wrote years later at the time of CK's death: "I'll always remember him with fondness. I remember him catching grasshoppers and then showing us how to use them to catch fish in the creek. I remember picking corn, mowing the lawn, and carrying desks because we liked him-- respected him. He was fun to work for. I remember when he took me to water the football stadium and we stopped at the post office. I remember him bunting and beating it out to the clothesline pole that was first base in Mamommy's backyard. Most of all, I remember him sitting at the table on the porch with corn on the cob and a large glass of iced tea in front of him, playfully leading a discussion on the pros of Texas and the cons of New Mexico."

Bob's brother Rick said that "When I think of him, I remember playing baseball in my Mamommy's backyard. He was happy and had a talent for making everyone around him happy. I respected C. K. very much and he has always been and will continue to be an example for me in the right way to live."

CK was a thrifty man and a handy man. His father, Charlie, was a carpenter and taught CK how to build. CK knew how to build a lot of things. His construction activities while in the south Pacific during World War II have already been noted. Not surprisingly, he continued those activities throughout his life.

There is no doubt that CK was handy but perhaps sometimes he got carried away. As CK's children got older, they came to expect the standard response *"I can make you one,"* whenever they needed something. Sometimes, it also meant that he could facilitate a cheaper solution instead of building or buying the needed commodity. One area where this was applied was pets.

Here are a couple of examples of how this procedure worked.

Debbie: "Daddy can I have a goldfish? "

CK : "Why sure sweetheart let's go down to the creek. We can get some goldfish there."

Back they came with golden tinted minnows and tadpoles soon to be frogs. Really, how many children grew up with goldfish that turned into frogs and hopped away from the aquarium?

Debbie: "Daddy can we have a rabbit?"

CK: "Sure, I think so".

And as soon as we saw a rabbit cross the road, CK would slam on the car brakes.

CK: "Charlie, catch that rabbit."

Charlie would bolt out of the back seat and go chasing through the tall grass after the rabbit. Charlie denies catching a rabbit, but Debbie remembers that he did. Everyone was surprised when he caught it, even CK. By the next morning, the rabbit had escaped, maybe with a little help.

Marj participated in one of the most spectacular *"I can make you one"* events.   Marj said that she wanted a birdbath positioned so that she could stand at the kitchen window, look out, and watch the birds playing in the birdbath. Marj received the standard "I can make you one" response when discussing her desire for a birdbath. True to his word CK went about assembling the birdbath materials – concrete, an 18" x 12" barrel, and a tin pie plate. He filled the barrel with concrete and pushed the pie plate in the top to make a slight indentation in the concrete. Once revealed, the finished result was a solid cylinder of concrete that weighed approximately 50 pounds with a slight indentation of about 2 inches in the top. This was not what Marj had envisioned. On a positive note, Debbie liked to push the birdbath over, stand on it and roll it across the yard. (Similar to log rolling). Debbie thought Marj might enjoy seeing her roll across the yard on the birdbath instead of birds splashing playfully in the water. We are happy to report that the bird bath did not fall on any birds killing them as they bathed or at least none while Marj was looking out the window.

Another incident with "I'll make it" overtones was Debbie's haircut. When she was small, most of the time it was her mother's job to get Debbie dressed and ready to go somewhere. Debbie rode to school with her mother and did not get up until after CK had left for school. In the summer, Debbie slept until she woke up. She had long hair that she usually wore in a ponytail. Every morning Debbie's mother would brush her hair and put it up. Both mother and daughter knew how the ponytail system worked. They both understood that Debbie was "tender-headed", although truthfully her sensitivity probably had more to do with how hard Debbie played and the tangles that she got in her hair rather than with any undue sensitivity. Debbie was too young to put her hair up, and if it were left down, it would turn into an even bigger mess. However, if the stylist pulled too hard while trying to put it up, Debbie would begin to cry loudly. Usually the howling, sobbing cries of distress were accompanied by an emphatic announcement that "You are pulling my hair! It hurts!"

During the summer after Debbie finished the first grade, her mother was away for a couple of weeks attending a United Methodist Women School of Missions course. That left CK responsible for the ponytail. Marj's day of departure was fine because she put up the ponytail; however, the second day, with CK on duty, was a disaster with crying and wailing. CK was not a big fan of crying and wailing. The third day was even worse, and the situation deteriorated with each new day. Both CK and Debbie dreaded the ponytail ordeal. Then, CK carefully engineered an innovative solution.

Each day CK talked about a new hair style called the "pixie cut" and about how nice Debbie would look with a pixie cut. Debbie, having a child's respect for her father, soon agreed to try the new hair style.

At the beauty shop, Mrs. Welch, the hairdresser, confirmed repeatedly with CK that the family really wanted that much hair cut off and that such a drastic change would be acceptable to Debbie's mother. CK assured Mrs. Welch that all was in order so Debbie skipped out of the beauty shop with a pixie cut, and morning styling became a painless breeze. CK was quite pleased with this outcome and complimented Debbie every day until Marj came home.

When her mother pulled into the driveway, Debbie rushed out to meet her and to show Marj her new hair style. Marj had a funny look on her face, but she agreed that the pixie cut looked good. Many years later her mother admitted to Debbie that when she first saw Debbie, she thought, "My baby. My baby's beautiful hair, what have they done to you? " It took two years for Debbie's hair to grow back.

Debbie several months after the haircut

According to CK's daughter, the bandmaster of the Crawford High School band had the band play *Anchors Away* as the musicians left the football field after their halftime performance in recognition of CK's World War II navy service.

There is a story, possibly apocryphal or improbably enlarged, that soon after CK and his family moved to Crawford, some high school boys determined to play a prank on them. The boys planned to approach CK's house and take off the front door screen to scare the family. As things developed, CK got wind of the students' plans, and he and Marj worked out a response. On the appointed night, when the boys approached the house, Marj feigned fright and held their attention while CK went out the back door, circled around the house, and concealed himself in the boys' car. As they were driving away chortling over their success, CK rose up from the back seat and scared them witless. There were no more such pranks attempted.

Around about 1960, CK's family was given a mixed-breed terrier puppy by Garrett Sparkman. Naturally, we had to name the dog. CK Junior was in his Civil War phase and wanted to name the puppy "Stonewall Jackson."

Debbie held out for something more traditional, like "Tip" from her first grade reader. The two siblings battled over several days using all their persuasive powers but could not reach an agreement. Finally, CK set a deadline for them to decide on a name with him to make the selection if they could not. The deadline passed with no name, so CK announced that the dog would be called "Hushpuppy."

Everyone agreed that Hushpuppy was an admirable name, but there was one problem. Hush was an alert little watchdog who would bark and growl ferociously when anyone approached our house. We would silence him by yelling "Hush!" If our visitors were not acquainted with Hushpuppy, they frequently thought we were ordering them to be silent--not the most cordial way to initiate interaction.

From my vantage point, it appeared that CK had a close relationship with his cousin Jake Bonds. Jake was the son of Pap Burns' sister, Jenny Burns Bonds. He and CK were about the same age and had both been in World War II, both in the Pacific theater as I recall. Jake was a football official and worked many Crawford games, especially on Thursday nights when no one else was playing. Crawford fans were always happy to see Jake as one of the officials because he was a good one. Jake was about the same size as CK with a smooth bald head and a big booming laugh. When our families visited, Jake would always ask me to do some tricks. Normally I would have been too shy to do that, but Jake was a good friend to CK and that made it acceptable to perform some simple tricks. Whatever I did, Jake would give it his stamp of approval with a big belly laugh.

Whenever the family traveled by car, CK drove. Marj was a perfectly competent driver, but CK drove. In those days, that was simply the way the universe was ordered: men drove. The children sat in the back seat and were left to amuse themselves except for those times that CK requested a neck rub. Sometimes Marj would reach across the seat and administer the necessary treatment, but it was done better and more effectively by the child sitting directly behind CK. We seldom made a trip of any appreciable distance that did not require one or more neck rubs for the driver.

After a few years as superintendent, the school board authorized the purchase of a car for CK to use for travel on school business. While Charlie lived at home, there were two "school cars," first a 1949 Ford and then a 1951 or 1952 Ford. Later, around 1969, there was a more presentable vehicle. All were purchased as government surplus cars. They were bereft of any creature comforts, and two of them had holes in the floorboard so that riders could see the ground flashing by. CK was very particular that only he drive the school cars since they were intended for school business. In the beginning, the school car was always parked on the side of the street in front of the house. One always knew that if the school car was gone, CK was not at home.

CK was not a master chef; however, he was a more than adequate fry cook. He made a nice fried okra and potato dish and a tasty chicken fried steak. His children were less fond of his fried egg sandwiches and his fried cornbread seasoned with bacon and onions and dunked in milk.

CK did have some favorite foods including sweets of all kinds, chicken fried steak, and fried chicken. In regard to fried chicken, CK said that wings were his favorite part of a chicken because that is what had been left to him growing up--and I can attest that he enjoyed wings all his adult life as well. As a child I saw him choosing to eat fried chicken wings so I thought they must be very special, but I could never get one when CK was at the table. He also mentioned that he got watermelon for his birthday because his birthday was in the summer time.

Regardless of the menu there were a couple rules to be observed at CK's table. No shirtless males or reading were allowed there. The shirt requirement was not a burdensome one, but the reading prohibition occasionally galled the other three family members all of whom were avid readers. Anytime CK missed a meal with his family, the books were sure to appear at the table.

As a child Charlie had a fondness for little toy soldiers, and he would request them as a gift every Christmas. One year CK decided it would be fun to stand the toy soldiers in the garden and shoot at them with a BB gun from Charlie's bedroom. The two marksmen took the screen off a bedroom window, lay down across the bed, and fired away. They both thought it was great fun (Do not think about this incident too rigorously. The soldiers were small and the distance to the targets was relatively long so that it is difficult now to imagine how the shooters actually saw the toy soldier targets--but this is the way Charlie remembers the event.).

Mention has already made of CK's repeated Sunday morning admonitions to his son to speak to people entering church and of Charlie's shortcomings in this area. But perhaps there was a certain familial predisposition toward a bit of shyness or reluctance to let people get too close that contributed to Charlie's difficulty in speaking to people. Interestingly enough in later years Charlie noted that CK kept many new acquaintances at some length as well. When he introduced himself, he would usually say "Burns is my name," which left the other person no choice but to refer to him as Mr. Burns and not as CK.

When CK was taking courses for a master's degree at Baylor in the early 1950's, Marj and Charlie sometimes accompanied him to Waco to shop while he was in class. If things worked out just right, the family could have a breakfast of an Orange Julius drink and spudnuts which were doughnuts made with potato flour. Then, after CK's class was over, the family could go to Youngblood's Restaurant for a lunch of hot, greasy fried chicken with rolls and honey. No doubt there were vegetable side dishes available, but they were not the reason we went to Youngblood's.

Popcorn was one of CK's favorite snacks, usually to be eaten while watching television in the evening. Apparently CK enjoyed popcorn all his life because he mentions eating it at Bessie Nowlin's boarding house in his wartime letters to Marj. There was nothing fancy about the preparation of CK's popcorn. He made it in a cast iron skillet over a gas stove. When the oil got hot, the cook shook the skillet vigorously while the corn popped. When it stopped popping, it was time to eat.

When CK Jr. was about five years old, CK would let him drive the car on the way to visit Celia is Valley Mills. Jr. would sit in CK's lap and hold the steering wheel and guide the car while CK worked the pedals. Naturally Jr. was closely monitored, but he still thought he was very big, and driving was great fun.

When CK Jr. was about six years old, he began collecting bottle caps. This was before aluminum cans were used, so there were plenty of bottle caps available. Initially Jr. collected only clean, neat bottle caps and only one of each variety. However, Jr. soon exhausted the supply of different bottle caps, so he began to collect more than one example of the various brands. At the same time, he began to add beer bottle caps to his inventory, and he became much less squeamish about gathering in dirty, nasty bottle caps. Soon he had a large cardboard box full of smelly, disgusting bottle caps. That would not have been such a bad thing except that his collection typically traveled with him--and with the family. When Jr. was not traveling, the collection stayed in the house in Jr.'s room.

Jr.'s parents were not pleased with his choice of hobbies and soon tired of his reeking box of bottle caps, but they foresaw resistance if they simply ordered him to get rid of his collection. CK took the matter into his capable hands. One afternoon, while driving to Valley Mills, he announced casually that he thought it would be fun to throw some bottle caps out of the window. He asked Jr. what he thought. Jr. always thought that his father's ideas were good, so he agreed, and father and son began tossing bottle caps out of the car. In order not to alarm Jr., CK soon stopped throwing out bottle caps and suggested that they could do some more on the next trip to Valley Mills. And they did. They threw out bottle caps on every trip until the collection had been completely dispersed.

Mention has already been made of CK's competitive nature. This approach to life also applied to games and contests with family members. CK cut a person no slack merely because they were his wife or his children. When Junior was about fourteen, he had surgery and had to spend a few days in the hospital. His hospital stay came just at a time when he was learning to play chess. CK saw what Junior was doing and asked if he could play. Junior was happy to oblige, and since he knew a little more about the game than did CK, he won the first few matches. CK was a perfectly loving father in that setting, but he still did not like to lose. He continued to play and to hone his skill and knowledge until he could beat Junior at will. Then he abandoned the game and as far as is known never played again.

Fall of 1969

CK and Marj and their children enjoyed life in Crawford. In many ways it was an ideal existence that allowed the family to savor the serenity and peace of small-town life while the adults went about making their corner of the world a better place for all. However, most regrettably and unfortunately, CK was struck down prematurely by cancer. What follows are the recollections of those last days by Debbie who was on the scene. CK Jr. was away in the army.

It was the fall of 1969. School had begun, and Crawford was in the midst of football season. Charlie had enlisted in the army that summer and was at Ft. Sill in Oklahoma. The rest of us were caught up in school fall activities. Charlotte, Charlie's wife, was the fourth-grade teacher in Crawford. I was a sixteen-year-old junior. Little did we realize that our world was about to be turned upside down.

Except for an ulcer, I cannot remember Daddy ever being sick, complaining about health issues, or going to the doctor. However, in October, he went to the doctor in Valley Mills because he felt so bad. The doctor found nothing.

I knew that Daddy was not feeling well. I can remember the weekend before he was hospitalized whining about something as teenagers do, and he asked me to stop because he felt bad. He didn't say it in a firm way or an angry way, but something about what he said unnerved me, enough so that I stopped right away and so that I still remember the incident more than 50 years later. This was my first clue of what was to come.

Mother and Daddy always drove separate cars to school. Daddy went to school early and stayed until football practice was over. Mother and I went an hour or so later and came home somewhere between 3:30 and 4:00. On non-game days, the football team practiced from about 2:30 to about 5:30 at the practice field at school.

It was a Tuesday. We all went to school, and during the day, Daddy was taken to the hospital and admitted. I am not sure how he got to the hospital. My guess is that Mother took him. Daddy was taken to the Goodall-Witcher Hospital in Clifton, Texas and admitted on October 14, 1969.

According to Burns family custom, I was sent to school the next day. Mother was at the hospital. At this point, people in Crawford thought everything would be okay. I did not think that. I felt it was more serious, not like the ulcer Daddy had suffered some years earlier. He was not getting better.

Skeet Dansby, Daddy's cousin, was a respected Registered Nurse at the Clifton hospital, and I think she helped to expedite Daddy's care. After a couple of days in Clifton, Daddy was moved to Scott & White Hospital in Temple because that facility was better equipped to handle his case. On

123

October 16 or 17, he was moved by ambulance to Scott & White. At this point there was no diagnosis, and he was in a regular hospital room.

From a logistical standpoint the move to Scott & White was helpful to the family since Mother's mother, Louise Jones, lived in Temple. Mother would have a place where she could change clothes, get a bite to eat, and rest for a short while, although in reality she spent almost all her time at the hospital with Daddy.

When Daddy was moved to Scott & White, I stayed with LeRoy & Shorty Mappe. Someone would take me to the hospital on the weekends. I think I even went to the football games since I was in the band. I can remember being asked by Mr. Allen, the band director, how my Dad was doing. I just stood there looking at him and shaking my head back and forth. I think that I finally mumbled, "not good."

One day during the week of October 26, I was called out of chemistry class and told to bring all my things with me. I was sent to the office where Shorty Mappe was waiting for me. Shorty told me that my Father was having a heart attack and that we were driving to the hospital. She hoped that she got me there in time. She left unspoken the definition of "in time for what?" but I understood. It was the longest car ride of my life, and I am sure it was difficult for Shorty with a 16-year-old weeping beside her.

When we got to the hospital, we found that Daddy had survived the heart attack which had been caused by a blood clot moving through his heart.

124

Around this time Daddy was diagnosed with multiple myeloma, a cancer that forms in white blood cells.

At this point Mother and Daddy knew there was no cure. The doctors told Mother that Daddy was alive only because of his willpower and his determination to fight. Later that week, Daddy told Mother that he could not fight any more.

The Red Cross was called to facilitate "compassionate leave" for Charlie to come home from Ft. Sill for 72 hours. Mother told me that I needed to go back to Crawford and go to school. I refused. I told Mother that I would not go back to Crawford and that she could not make me. My friend, Donna Steinke, could bring my homework to me and I would do it in Temple. We settled the matter with an agreement that I would stay in Temple but that I would not visit Daddy during school hours or tell him I was staying in Temple because he would be upset that I was missing school.

We stayed at Grandmother Jones' house in Temple. Charlie arrived. He and Charlotte spent the first night sleeping on the floor in the living room. Then they moved to a hotel across the highway from the hospital. Charlotte would go each day and teach her fourth grade class in Crawford. Mother, Charlie, and I would go to the hospital each day. Mother and Charlie would go into Daddy's room and I would sit in the waiting room until after 4:30 or 5:00, time enough for me to have been in school and then driven to Temple. Charlie left after three days knowing that he would not see our Father alive again.

After Charlie left, Mother's sister, Clada Brumley, came from Houston. She was with Mother every step of the remaining way, something for which I will be eternally grateful. She allowed Mother and Daddy time to talk and say their goodbyes without interruption.

When Daddy's prognosis became publicly known, people started to come. Daddy was in intensive care with visitors allowed 5 minutes every hour. The hospital soon waived this restriction and let people into the room every 5 minutes. Once the workday was over, people would start showing up each day. They would line up down the hall waiting to visit. One of our family would be in the room with Daddy and the visitor. The visitor's register recorded 222 people who came in person to the hospital during the period from October 25 through November 3.

Daddy told me I was the best daughter in the world, and I told him he was the best Daddy in the world.

He died early in the morning at 6:58 AM on Wednesday, November 5, 1969.

The Goodbye

Early the morning CK died, Marj was called to the hospital. Clada went with her. They left Debbie asleep, unaware that her father had died. They returned to the Jones residence about 8:30. Debbie awoke to hear Clada on the telephone with the Red Cross requesting their assistance in arranging another 72-hour compassionate leave for Charlie so he could return home for the funeral.

Marj, Clada, and Debbie quickly packed and left Temple to return to Crawford. On the way home, they stopped at Cole Funeral Home in McGregor. Clada and Marj left Debbie in the car under a shade tree and went in to finalize funeral arrangements, many of which had probably already been made.

By the time the women returned to Crawford, the news of CK's death had begun to spread. Very soon people began appearing at the house to drop off food for the family, to offer condolences and to provide the comfort of their presence. People came and went the entire day.

Funeral plans must have been made in advance because events moved very quickly. The visitation was scheduled to take place at Cole Funeral Home that night, November 5. The funeral was set for the next day at 3:00 pm at the Methodist Church in Crawford. School was cancelled so that everyone could attend.

There was a realistic concern that the Crawford Methodist Church would not be able to accommodate the crowd that was expected, even though chairs were placed in the aisles, the large reception hall, the foyer, and upstairs. Someone had the foresight to wire the Baptist Church across the street for sound so that people could sit there and hear the service. The funeral address was given by Rev. Jerry Walters, the local Baptist minister and a good friend of CK's. He was assisted by Rev. Rollo Herrington, the Crawford Methodist minister at the time, and by Rev. J. E. Morton, a former Crawford Methodist minister and friend. There were eight pallbearers:

Jack Allen: Crawford school band director
Jack Ramsey: next door neighbor and friend
Milton Fulp: friend and school board member
Ira Gohlke: friend and school board president
Franklin Hodel: neighbor and school board member
LeRoy Mappe: neighbor and school board member
G. H. "Sparky" Sparkman: friend and school co-worker
Clifford Noland: friend and school board member

Members of the football team were asked to serve as honorary pallbearers.

Except for the number of people in attendance, it is difficult to remember much about the funeral. The memories come as snapshots:

- the overflow of the crowd to the Baptist Church
- the entry to the church past the football team lined up in their black letter jackets
- sitting at the front on the right-hand side

- watching as the community slowly moved past the casket for a final goodbye
- the hushed, respectful silence of the crowd waiting for the family to emerge from the church

And, the procession on the drive back to CK's home--to Valley Mills--the place his life began.

Appreciation

There was an outpouring of love and respect for CK from the community and from the wider central Texas area. Despite the fact that the total population of Crawford was 423 people, over 675 people signed the funeral registration book. More than 100 floral arrangements were sent to the funeral service including some from neighboring school districts such as Axtell, Valley Mills, McGregor, Bruceville-Eddy, Clifton, and Robinson. Almost 200 donations were made in memory and in honor of CK.

Over the next several weeks tributes continued to be received by the family such as the ones below:

"He just seemed to be a fellow that was willing to help anyone in any way that he could and I appreciated knowing a man like him."

"I have often said that of all the superintendents and coaches in our area, I appreciated and liked none quite so much as I did Mr. Burns, as a matter of fact he was appreciated by our entire community. I know that the term 'Gentleman' is often used loosely but the expression, and all the good things that it implies could be fully applied to Mr. Burns."

"I shall always remember him as the coach, teacher, counselor and for the special interest he had in our bond. He was my ideal and friend."

"I shall be grateful for the rest of my life to Mr. Burns. He gave me a wonderful guidance in those most important years now behind me. He set an inspiring example for all of us."

"...the many lives he has touched and the good influence he has had on so many."

"How thankful we are that he was part of our boys' lives."

"He was a wonderful friend, the example he set is appreciated more and more each day."

"I know of no one whom I had greater respect and confidence or enjoyed working with, or for, than I did Mr. Burns."

Life Goes On

By Friday, November 7, school was back in session with a football game in Lorena that night. The game was played because CK would have wanted it that way.

By Monday, November 10, Charlie was back at Ft. Sill, and Marj and Debbie were back in school, beginning a painful and surreal life without CK.

After CK's death, Charlie returned to Crawford only for visits. Marj continued to teach at Crawford until she retired in 1975. She lived in Crawford until she moved to Waco some years later. Debbie graduated from Crawford High School and lived in Crawford until she was 22 then returned only for visits.

As for CK, his legacy has lived on. His was a life well lived, and we, his children, are grateful and appreciative to have been a part of that wonderful life.

Postscript

Some years after CK died, his children were encouraging their mother to expand her social activities and to enter into romantic relationships and even to remarry if she so chose. Marj listened for a while to the unsolicited and naive advice of her children and then quietly observed, "If you've had the best, you don't need the rest." CK Burns was indeed the best.

By: Watson

SENATE RESOLUTION NO. 396

In Memory
of
Mr. Charles K. Burns

WHEREAS, Charles K. Burns of Crawford, Texas, a prominent civic leader and one of Texas' outstanding high school coaches, died Wednesday, November 5, 1969, at the age of 57; and

WHEREAS, Mr. Burns coached football at Crawford High School for the past 24 years and under his leadership the team won 184 games out of 252 played and won district championships 11 times during the past 14 years; and

WHEREAS, In one stretch the distinguished coach put championships back-to-back for ten years to win 48 district games with only one loss, a gridiron record which still stands as one of the finest ever compiled in Texas football; his Crawford teams amassed 15 district championships, 6 bi-district championships, and 3 regional titles; and

WHEREAS, A graduate of Valley Mills High School, Mr. Burns attended North Texas State College and was co-captain of the Eagles football team during his senior year; earning the name "Elongated End" for his pass catching ability; and

WHEREAS, After graduation in 1939, he began his coaching career at Valley Mills High School and then moved to El Paso in 1942, teaching school for several months before joining the Navy and serving for four years in the Pacific theater; and

WHEREAS, Mr. Burns also served as Crawford School superintendent for 24 years, and his dedication to academic excellence as well as athletic prowess made him one of Crawford's most respected and distinguished citizens; now, therefore, be it

RESOLVED, That the Senate of the 62nd Legislature honor the memory of Charles K. Burns and extend sympathy to the members of his family: his wife, Mrs. Marjorie Jones Burns; his son, Charles K. Burns, Jr. of Ft. Sill, Oklahoma; and to his daughter, Deborah Burns of Crawford; and, be it further

RESOLVED, That copies of this Resolution be prepared for the members of his family; and that when the Senate of the State of Texas adjourns today it do so in his memory.

Ben Barnes
Lieutenant Governor

I hereby certify that the above Resolution was adopted by the Senate on February 17, 1971, by a rising vote.

Charles Schnabel
Secretary of the Senate

www.ingramcontent.com/pod-product-compliance
Lightning Source LLC
Chambersburg PA
CBHW040858100426
42813CB00015B/2840